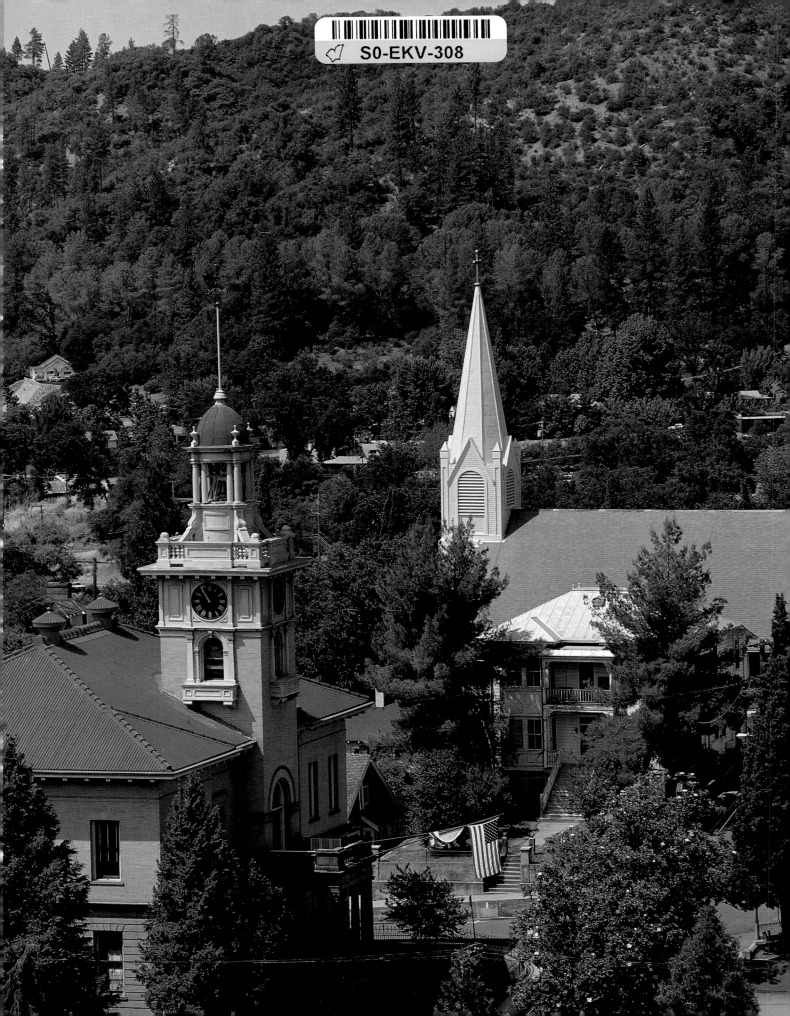

SO-EKV-308

The Story Of GOLD COUNTRY CALIFORNIA

Written, designed and edited
by
Adam R. Collings

Mechanicals
by
Kacy L. Tribble

Photography
by
Ed Cooper and Mark Gibson

Published by
GOLD MOUNTAIN BOOKS
P.O. Box 482
Lake Arrowhead, CA 92352

Printed in China
by
Palace Press International

ISBN 0-933692-99-1

ⓒ1996 Adam Randolph Collings

Library of Congress Catalog Card Number : 96-096123

California Bound

Front Cover: *Stately Placer County Courthouse and monument to the forty-niner/Auburn (Photo by Ed Cooper).*
Back Cover: *Historic Gold Rush Structure at Shingle Springs (Photo by Ed Cooper).*
Frontispiece: *Sonora/Capitol City of the Southern Mines (Photo by Ed Cooper). Sutter's Mill/Gold Discovery Site (Photo by Ed Cooper). Engineer's Office at the Empire Mine/Grass Valley (Photo by Mark Gibson).*
Last Page: *Coloma (Photo by Mark Gibson).*

Contents

Forty-Niner

Not a road atlas or historical tome, but rather an exhilarating romp through California's Gold Country, this handsome publication has been produced to deliver hours of educational entertainment for both the arm chair traveler and the "Indiana Jones."

The California Gold Rush was in fact a grand, gaudy adventure for a generation of young people. With literally thousands of stories having been told and retold, there remains hardly a reference unchallenged by Gold Rush historians and aficionados. In our telling of this remarkable saga, we have made every effort to ensure accuracy of all information presented without making any claim to settle that which the experts never will. We assume no liability in the event of errors. Whenever possible, permission has been obtained for use of art, graphics and photography. In a number of cases, however, locating ownership has proven "impossible." We have made every effort to obtain permissions as required.

Enjoy!

Publisher
Gold Mountain Books

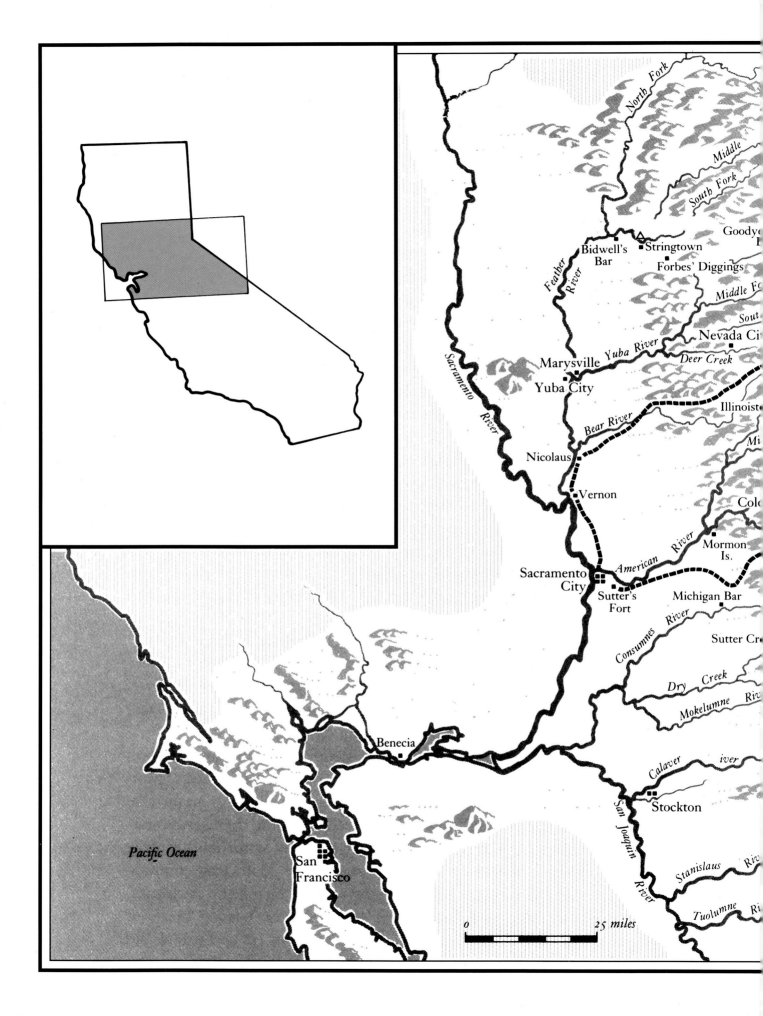

North Fork

Middle

South Fork

Goodye

Bidwell's
Bar
Stringtown
Forbes' Diggings

Feather
River

Middle F

Sout

Nevada Ci

Marysville
Yuba River
Deer Creek

Yuba City

Illinoist

Sacramento
River

Bear River

Mi

Nicolaus

Vernon

Col

American
River

Mormon
Is.

Sacramento
City

Sutter's
Fort
Michigan Bar

Consumnes River
Sutter Cr

Dry Creek

Mokelumne Riv

Benecia

Calaver
iver

Stockton

Pacific Ocean

San Joaquin
River

San
Francisco

Stanislaus Riv

Tuolumne Ri

0   25 miles

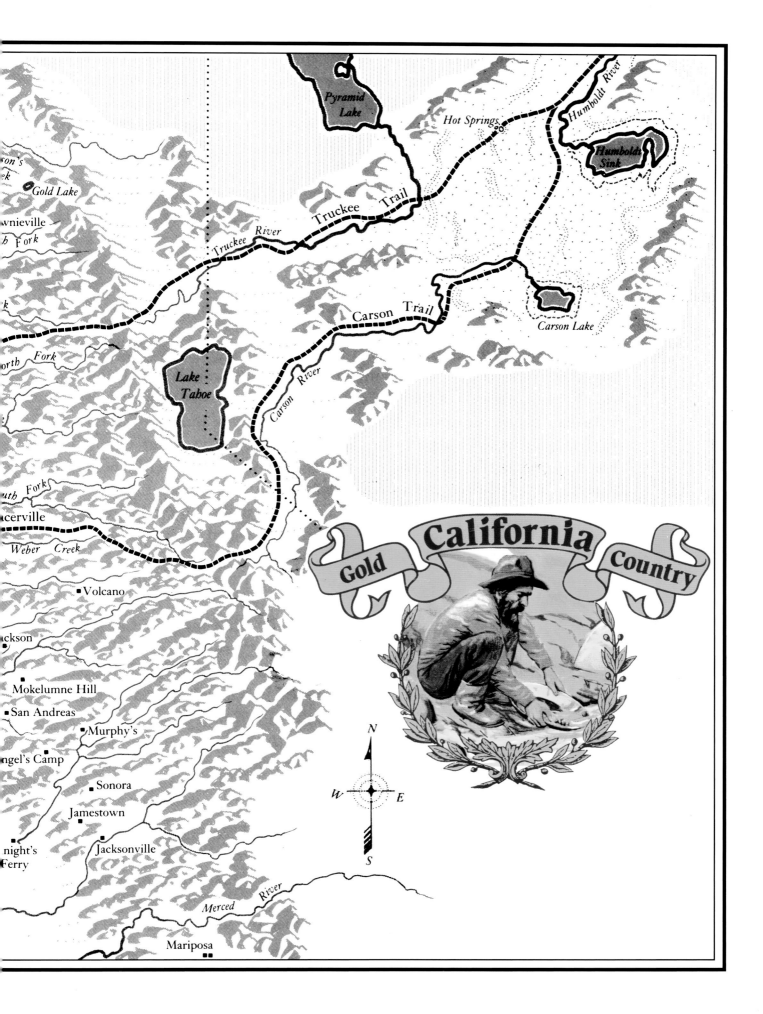

Pyramid
Lake

Humboldt River

Hot Springs

Humboldt
Sink

son's
eek

Gold Lake

wnieville

h Fork

Truckee Trail

Truckee River

Truckee

k

Carson Trail

Carson Lake

orth Fork

Lake
Tahoe

Carson River

uth Fork

cerville

Weber Creek

Volcano

ckson

Mokelumne Hill

San Andreas

Murphy's

ngel's Camp

Sonora

Jamestown

night's
Ferry

Jacksonville

Merced River

Mariposa

Gold **California** *Country*

N
W — E
S

Prologue

Two hundred million years ago North America's Pacific Coast roughly paralleled its contemporary configuration, although at the time it lay some four hundred miles further south and east, nearly along what is now the western boundary of the state of Nevada.

Under the ocean, off the coast of present-day Nevada, unprecedented features of a unique landscape were beginning to take shape. Volcanic action produced mammoth mountains laced with veins of gold. They pushed skyward to form two gigantic and distinct massifs, each running parallel to the other, as the Pacific's heavy rock floor began to slide under the lighter, granite core of the North American continent.

From an arc of offshore islands, both ranges were forced ever upward until eventually they and their splendid mineral-laden valleys came to lie wholly above the level of the sea.

During the eons that followed, an emerald cloak descended upon the new land as forests of redwood, pine, and fir advanced southward from what is today the Pacific Northwest. In the valleys rich grasses and herbs began to grow. Over a dozen varieties of oak took root on her thousand hills, while fan palms sprouted in the more arid canyon regions to the east.

California Jaguar

Hundreds of thousands of animals moved into this lush paradise, as did man himself. At the dawning of modern times scores of native American tribal groups co-existed peacefully amidst vast roaming herds of elk, deer, and antelope. Man's only true challenge for pre-eminence in this new coastal province came from the jaguar, the panther, and the great grizzly bear.

European eyes, when first they beheld this new land in the fall of 1542, spoke of it with a tone of marked familiarity; for although they had only now seen it for the first time it had in fact existed in the minds of Europeans for many centuries. From as far back as the dark ages poets and minstrels had spoken of just such a place. In the legends of Iberia this terrestrial paradise had been given the name of California, after a legendary female *caliph*, or queen, who was said to have ruled over it. So it was that Juan Rodriguez Cabrillo, Portuguese maritimer sailing under the flag of Spain, recognized before him, as he gazed out across the torrey pines and azure waters of San Diego Bay, the mythical land incarnate as it rose up before him. He and his crew made reference to California in their ship's log as though it had always been that self-same California of legend. No doubt they fully expected, if fortune be in their favor, to encounter the rich kingdoms of gold that were purported to lie perhaps just beyond those distant purple mountain ranges.

Miwok Indian

The Spaniards never found the caliph, nor her riches; although this land that they had "discovered" would indeed yield more gold than all the Latin American conquests of Cortez and Pizarro combined.

Spain laid claim to California as her own. England's renegade pirate Sir Francis Drake would challenge that claim in 1579, even attempting to rename it New England (Nova Albion). But the Iberian monarchs would prevail, and in 1769 what came to be known as the Sacred Expedition ushered in one of the most colorful and romantic eras of western American history.

Gaspar de Portola, newly appointed governor of the California frontier, in company with Father Junipero Serra, a devout Franciscan and former president of the Mexico City Missionary College, set out to conquer and colonize the great northern mystery, as it had come to be called. Anticipating encounters with griffins and amazons, they found instead a humble, peace-loving people; many of whom at first heralded their arrival as a sign from heaven.

Between 1769 and 1823 some twenty-one mission outposts were established up and down the California coast. Today these beautiful relics evoke to the minds of residents and visitors alike idyllic images of a not-so-distant past. On September 27, 1821, Mexico declared its independence from Spain. The proud Franciscans refused allegiance to the newly-founded revolutionary regime and were subsequently expelled. Eight million acres of mission lands fell into the hands of the fledgling Mexican government. In exchange for military service and political favors, Mexico City parceled out the grand old Franciscan dynasty to some eight hundred would-be rancheros. A feudal-type system, built largely upon the backs of Indian slave labor, came to exist. From their grand haciendas this newly-landed gentry ruled over prolific cattle-ranching empires.

Sir Francis Drake

In his book *Two Years Before the Mast*, Yankee adventurer-turned-novelist Richard Henry Dana told of how cattle hides (commonly referred to at the time as California banknotes) were bartered with passing ships for the comforts of the Eastern seaboard. American traders grew rich and powerful as did the Spanish land barons they illegally traded with (Mexico having forbidden the importation of American goods). California became a virtual suburb of New England.

The romantic rancho era had begun. Amid such bounty and natural beauty the much-sought-after California lifestyle of today was born - a tradition marked by gracious hospitality and the endless pursuit of pleasure. Yes, there was work to be done. Yet from its inception the Californian's daily routine has been seasoned with copious amounts of time alloted for recreation and leisure. Bull fights, rodeos, and colorful fiestas with music and fandango dancing were just a few of these earliest indulgences.

Spanish Caravel

It was during the height of this rancho era that California's cache of gold was at last discovered. The year was 1842. Francisco Lopez, while out rounding up stray horses, paused to take a siesta under what has since come to be known as the Oak of the Golden Dream. The old oak shaded an arroyo (small stream) not far from the ruins of Mission San Fernando in Los Angeles. Lopez, using his knife to uproot and prepare some wild onions for eating, discovered, attached to their roots,

Johann A. Sutter

John Wilson Marshall

a small nugget of gold. The rather insignificant vein thus discovered soon played out, however, and nothing more was made of the incident.

In the meantime Washington had become aware of this West Coast land of milk and honey. As early as 1826 American mountain men had breached the high Sierra barrier that effectively isolated California from the rapidly developing Yankee nation to the east. In the 1830's President Andrew Jackson had sent an emissary to Mexico City in an effort to entice that nearly bankrupt nation with an offer to purchase California for half a million dollars. The Mexicans were not interested. Undaunted, President James K. Polk vowed to acquire California "by any means". With British financial interests attempting to exchange $26 million in defaulted Mexican bonds for the rich lands of the West Coast, Washington stretched to interpret several isolated border incidents along the Rio Grande as a threat to national security. Hence, war was declared on Mexico, and within two years the United States laid claim to the whole of the American Southwest, including its crown jewel, Alta California.

The treaty of Guadalupe Hidalgo was signed into force on February 2, 1848. For the most part Californians accepted and indeed welcomed their new Yankee sovereigns, whose very presence had from the beginning brought them great wealth and prosperity. For a brief period of time life on the ranchos continued on, little changed.

Nearly a decade earlier, in 1839, a Swiss entrepreneur and self-proclaimed dignitary by the name of Johann Augustus Sutter had arrived in the Spanish port of San Francisco. The congenial gentleman quickly fell into favor with local Spanish authorities and, like so many of his Latin contemporaries, was granted title to his own rancho. Unlike his new-found neighbors, however, Sutter had asked for and received a tract of land so vast that he literally established his own "independent" barony. He called the estate New Helvetia after his homeland. His headquarters came to be known as Sutter's Fort, and it was to this splendid little principality that the earliest American emigrants had flocked.

Sutter gloried in providing much-needed comfort and goods (for a price, of course) to California's newest settlers. He was indeed a gracious host and a generous man. Nonetheless New Helvetia turned an enviable profit, and he soon began investing in far-flung enterprises, one of which would come to inaugurate the single most significant event in the history of what was soon to become known as the "State" of California.

In 1847 Sutter hired one James Wilson Marshall, an American, to oversee the construction of a sawmill on the American River. On January 24, 1848, nine days before the United States would actually acquire the territory from Mexico, Marshall, while inspecting the nearly completed project, observed a bit of shiny material in the mill's tailrace. "Monday 24th" wrote Mormon laborer Henry W. Bigler, "this day some kind of mettle was found in the tail race that looks like goald first discovered by James Martial, the boss of the mill." Marshall quietly took the suspect mineral to Sutter, who "applied every test of their ingenuity" to determine if the bright and malleable substance was in fact what they suspected it to be. It proved indeed to be "the finest kind of gold!" The two men raced back to the mill where they "poked and panned awhile." More "color" was produced. The stunned pair soon came to realize that they had indeed, by mere chance, stumbled upon the Caliph's hidden treasure. An American had "discovered" that which had eluded the Spaniard's for more than a century (California's much-sought-after cache of gold) ironically little more than a week before Iberia's child would cede all rights to the fortune over to the United States of America.

Sutter was quick to realize that New Helvetia would be overrun by fortune seekers if word of their discovery were to leak out. He swore his mill hands to secrecy. Nevertheless as nuggets began showing up at saloons and shops in the surrounding coastal mission towns the local populace became curious.

Sam Brannan

It was Sam Brannan, leader of San Francisco's large Mormon congregation, who caught on to Sutter's secret and "let the cat out of the bag." First, however, he established a well-stocked drygoods operation near the site of the mill. Then, with nuggets of gold in hand, he paraded up and down the streets of San Francisco shouting, "Gold! Gold on the American River!" Nothing could have held back the flood of humanity that followed. Literally speaking, the world came rushing in, as sailing vessels spread Brannan's announcement to the far-flung corners of the earth.

During the first three years of California's Gold Rush, more than two hundred fifty thousand men poured through San Francisco's Golden Gate or over the high passes of the Sierra Nevada mountains. This incredible tide of emigrants drastically altered Spanish California, serving as a catalyst for the foundation of a great West Coast empire. Sam Brannan became the territory's first millionaire, while John Sutter lost everything in the madness that ensued. On the site of New Helvetia came to stand the elegant capitol building; seat of government for the people of the State of California.

Forty-niners, as they came to be called, after the year in which the raucous began, spent their days hip deep in sand and gravel panning for gold, and their nights in revelry at the gambling halls and saloons that afforded them their only diversion. The majority being men in their early twenties, they were frequently preyed upon by the wordly-wise, with many a fortune being made and lost in a single day. It was not long before the tiny Spanish pueblo at San Francisco had become transformed into a thriving seaport metropolis. Built of redwood timbers upon a foundation of solid gold, in its unsurpassed Victorian extravagance San Francisco came to be heralded as a hallmark of Western civilization—the Paris of the New World. While mining activities focused on northern California, the rancheros of southern California were quick to cash in on their new-found market; supplying beef at vastly inflated prices to the flood of fortune seekers. During the course of the next decade, what with repeated gold strikes and subsequent funding for enterprise, both northern and southern California became collectively one of the wealthiest centers of civilization on earth; transformed quite literally overnight from a sylvan frontier to a cradle of opulence and industry.

Etching of the Forty-niners

13

A turn of the road presented a scene of mining life, as perfect in its details as it was novel in its features. Immediately beneath us the swift river glided tranquilly, though foaming still from the great battle which, a few yards higher up, it had fought with a mass of black obstructing rocks. On the banks was a village of canvas that the winter rains had leached to perfection and round it the miners were at work at every point. Many were waistdeep in the water, toiling in bands to construct a race and dam to turn the river's course; others were intrenched in holes, like grave-diggers, working down to the "bed rock". Some were on the brink of the stream washing out "prospects" from tin pans or wooden "batteas", and others worked in company with the long tom, by means of water-sluices artfully conveyed from the river. Many were coyote-ing in subterranean holes, from which from time to time their heads popped out, like those of squirrels, to take a look at the world, and a few with drills, dissatisfied with nature's work, were preparing to remove large rocks with gunpowder. All was life, merriment, vigor and determination, as this part of the earth was being turned inside out to see what it was made of.

-Francis James (Frank) Marryat,
Mountains and Molehills, or Recollections of a Burnt Journal (New York, 1855).

WASHING GOLD / CALAVERAS, CALIFORNIA

Artist unknown. © Laurie Platt Winfrey, Inc.

Used by permisson

California's Original State
Highway 49 Roadsign

Introduction

The term *Mother Lode* was originally coined to describe primarily one rich vein of California's gold ore. That vein was thought to have extended roughly 120 miles in length and a mile in width from Mariposa in the south, to Auburn in the north, along the gently rolling western slopes of California's rugged Sierra Nevada. It formed *the* focal point for mining activity and in fact was the scene of most of the action during the Gold Rush proper. There were, to be sure, rich diggings elsewhere throughout the Golden State but the Gold Rush Country considered herein is that which should properly be identified as the true *Mother Lode* itself together with what is correctly referred to as *The Northern Mines*; a geography of sweeping grasslands and handsome foothills and towering mountain peaks stretching roughly two hundred seventy miles between the communities of Coarsegold on the south and Vinton on the north.

It has been estimated that some 500 towns were born in this Gold Country between 1848 and 1860 as more than 300,000 emigrants flocked to California. Today fewer than half of these settlements remain, with many of those survivors being little more than a name on a signpost or historical monument. A handful have withstood the passage of time; some as centers of commerce and industry where new banks and commercial buildings often continue to be painstakingly constructed after the finest traditions of authentic Gold Rush architecture; others seemingly all but untouched by the advances of the 20th century, languishing in the charming glow of a bygone era. For the modern-day explorer, Gold Country today is traversed by, appropriately numbered, State Highway 49. Roughly tracing the legendary Mother Lode itself, most of the major mining camps are situated along or near this one singularly historic corridor.

Not unlike one vast *authentic* theme park, historic landmark towns and structures and signage literally lining Highway 49 (and its transportation tributaries) as it parades from one end of the Mother Lode to the other and beyond; perhaps the best way to explore Gold Country is to approach each section a day or two at a time.

Ranging in altitude from a few hundred feet above sea level to 6,670 foot pine and fir-clad, often snowy, Yuba Pass (with the granite spires of the Sierra Nevada, that gave birth to the gold-laden streams and rivers of the Mother Lode, ever present yet just out of sight, beyond the foothills you traverse), Highway 49 meanders at around 2,000 feet. Just north of Nevada City it turns eastward and climbs through the spectacular high Sierra itself.

Heading for the Gold Fields

16

In summer the weather along the Mother Lode is apt to be fiercely hot at lower elevations, but not surprisingly much more pleasant higher up in the timberbelt. With the arrival of autumn, fall foilage brightens the historic towns and cities with brilliant displays in amber, vermillion and gold. Winter rains bring renewal to the parched lowlands and snow to the high country. Spring covers the hillsides with wildflowers and the trees with new foliage while melting snow washes yet more gold dust loose, keeping the Gold Rush alive, albeit, as a mere whisper of its former self.

In addition to soaking up a little history residents and visitors alike enjoy indulging in what remains still a hedonist's paradise. Sampling fine wine at local vineyards, discovering a myriad of surviving saloons and historic restaurants, soaring over Gold Country in a hot air balloon, white water river rafting down the second most popular stretch of river for such sport in America, and, of course, panning for gold are but a few of this region's pleasurable offerings.

We invite you now to come and journey with us through this land that fostered many fortunes, many a dream-come-true *and* many a great adventure. . .

Forty-niner with Pan and Pickaxe

" Got a dream, boy, Got a song. Paint your wagon, and come along! "

-Alan Jay Lerner
"Paint Your Wagon"

Photo by Ed Cooper

THE MOTHER LODE: SOUTHERN DISTRICT

"This monument marks the southern terminus of Highway 49, which passes through 51 cities, towns and settlements and 11 counties in its 310-mile wandering route through some of the most scenic and mineral-rich area in all of the land." —Monument inscription in Oakhurst.

ur journey through California's fabled Gold Country begins just down the mountain from the alpine splendor of Yosemite National Park at a small hamlet known as COARSEGOLD.

Eight miles south of OAKHURST along State Highway 41, in what is today Madera County, COARSEGOLD became a thriving community overnight when prospectors began "picking up" nuggets of gold from the area's creek beds.

One of those nuggets, discovered by a group of argonauts (Greek for gold seekers) from Texas, tipped the scales at a value of $15,000 (in nineteenth century gold prices)!

Its discovery led to the establishment of the Texas Flats Mine; one of the most long-lived and extensively worked "hardrock" mines in the southern district. While "color" played out in COARSEGOLD by around 1890, the Texas Flats Mine continued to produce well into the 1900s. All that remains of that rich claim today is rubble and, perhaps, the elusive continuation of that particular vein of gold ore itself!

Little else survives in COARSEGOLD; a single false front, Gold Rush style building that today houses a saddle shop offering up western wear, and Yosemite Gallery, where native American crafts and jewelry as well as western art is showcased.

In the back country, off Highway 41, traveling through KNOWLES enroute to RAYMOND (formerly Wildcat Station), one notices a preponderance of stark stone foundations; silent monuments to buildings that have long since fallen victim to the passage of time. Garden walls and even fence posts here are made of stone.

It was, in fact, stone quarries in this area that produced much of the granite used to rebuild San Francisco following the devastating earthquake of 1906.

◆

At OAKHURST we reach the actual jumping off point for historic Highway 49. A monument bearing proclamation of such stands at the entrance to Raley's Shopping Center (near the junction of Highway 41 with Highway

LARAMORE-LYMAN HOME

PLACER MINING

19

49), an excellent point from which to provision for travels to all points beyond.

This area was originally called Fresno Flats. Its fortunes were nurtured by the stupendous wealth that flowed from nearby Enterprise Mine (which produced as much as $8 million in a single year). The fortunes of OAKHURST today are nurtured by the wealth that flows from a prolific tourist trade as the southern gateway to Yosemite National Park.

At the Fresno Flats Historical Park, a combined museum and outdoor gardens embrace an excellent collection of Gold Rush memorabilia together with an assortment of historic buildings. Primary among the latter is the beautiful Laramore-Lyman House.

Among the collections of the former we learn that the original Yosemite Sam was *not* a Warner Brothers looneytoon, but in fact a ranger who dedicated 40 years of his life to guarding the natural treasures of Yosemite National Park (his fine collection of western regalia being proudly displayed here).

Across the way, on a hill overlooking heavily traveled Highway 41 (just north of its juncture with 49) sits tiny but impressive Christs Church *and* an historic graveyard. Here among the weathered monuments we discover the final resting place of one Lieutenant Skeane S. Skeenes, who was killed in an encounter with Indians at nearby AHWAHNEE (it is not known how many native Americans were killed). Back at Highway 49 heading out north we leave, albeit only briefly, the traffic coursing

its way through town enroute to America's Switzerland to head out across the handsome oak-covered hill country that *is* the southernmost district of the storied Mother Lode.

Seven miles north of OAKHURST at AHWAHNEE sits the Wassama Roundhouse State Historic Park. Large ceremonial meeting houses constructed by the Miwok Indians, this particular roundhouse has been assembled on the site of a similar structure that was originally built during the Gold Rush in 1860. It serves today as focal point for a reconstructed Miwok village complete with cedar tepees, sweat house, and dance ring.

On a nearby hillside, above AHWAHNEE's post office, sits a sacred Indian burial ground.

At MORMON BAR nothing more than an historical marker remains to tell the story of the members of the Mormon Battalion (which had just completed the longest infantry march in history: from Council Bluffs, Iowa, to San Diego, where they arrived to find the war with Mexico—for which they had been recruited to fight—had ended), who came here to placer mine. The Mormons moved on to richer diggings elsewhere before dutifully returning to Utah to contribute their gold to the building of "Zion" in the Rocky Mountains.

Thousands of Chinese eventually worked through these same placers a second time; gleaning even more of the yellow "stuff that dreams are made of" from the rich paydirt abandoned by the Mormons.

STAMP MILL

Photo by Ed Cooper

"In the month of June, 1807, a party of (Spanish) Californians pitched their tents on a stream at the foot of the Sierra Nevada, and whilst there, myriads of butterflies, of the most gorgeous and variegated colors, clustered on the surrounding trees. . .from which circumstance they gave the stream the appellation of Mariposa (Spanish for butterfly)." —1850 California legislative report

s the scattered oak woodlands become crowded with pine you instinctively sense your approach to MARIPOSA and here discover the profound presence of Mother Lode history you may have felt missing amidst the new, albeit traditional Gold Rush style, commercial development and bustle of OAKHURST.

In MARIPOSA Main Street is lined with *authentic* Gold Rush structures: the sturdy stone Trabucco warehouse, wrought iron balconied Schlageter Hotel and false front Stolder Building (all still in operation, though not surprisingly, under *new* management).

Above this charming, history-rich town, rises the white-washed, steepled St. Josephs Catholic Church; beyond which stand outbuildings and tailing dumps of yet another *real* gold mine!

By all accounts MARIPOSA's crowning jewel is its classic Greek revival courthouse. In fact, the Mariposa County Courthouse, built in 1854, is the oldest continuously operating seat of government anywhere west of the Rocky Mountains: and what a vast, far-flung political district it once embraced. Frequently referred to by students of California history as the Mother of counties (Mother of all counties in popular vernacular), MARIPOSA at one time held jurisdiction over fully one fifth of what is today the State of California. From this noble little western courthouse with its classic clock tower, was governed an expanse of territory that reached from the central Mother Lode west to the Coast Range and south to what is now Lake Arrowhead and the San Bernardino Mountains (with a good share of the Mojave desert thrown in to boot)! Six *new* counties and segments of some five others would eventually be carved out of it, as post Gold Rush development led to rapid growth beyond this piney enclave. Many a landmark mining case came to be settled within the walls of this historic building at Tenth and Bullion Streets.

LEVI STRAUSS & CO.

Levi Strauss, the inventor of what many consider to be the quintessential American garment - the blue jean - was born in Bavaria, on February 26, 1829.

Levi together with his sister Fanny moved to San Francisco soon after receiving news of the California Gold Rush. He opened his first store, together with Fanny's husband David Stern, on California Street between Sansome and Battery in 1853.

Sometime after his arrival in San Francisco Levi hit upon the idea of making sturdy work pants out of some of the canvas material he had on hand. Whether he was asked to make the pants by the miners who frequented the city, or whether he observed that their trousers didn't hold up well in the diggings is not known. However they came about, his innovative work pants quickly became popular - especially after he took to the road as a peddler, traveling the small towns in the gold country. By the 1860s, Levi was buying denim from a mill in New Hampshire and his denim pants - known as "waist overalls" - became as popular as the original canvas variety.

Indeed, much of U.S. mining law is based upon decisions that were made here.

As was common throughout Gold Country, a fire, in 1866, all but destroyed MARIPOSA. The town survived for, as you soon realize if you haven't already, you are once again being joined here by the throngs headed for Yosemite, as Highway 140 bisects Highway 49. By the time the gold had played itself out the popularity of the grand natural cathedral of the high Sierra had flooded the town with trade in tourism.

While by no means the area's only industry, agricultural and logging interests as well as county government not withstanding, it is the travel trade that today continues to pump millions of dollars into Gold Country annually. You won't begrudge a single dollar invested as you linger; for when you depart you will discover that you have garnered some of this most historic of regions in the American West's intrinsic riches for yourself.

And MARIPOSA, in particular, is awash with such priceless gems. In addition to the aforementioned assortment of Gold Rush era architecture and a picturesque mountain setting and the alpine splendor of nearby Yosemite National Park, the town itself contains several outstanding cultural repositories. Principal among these is the Mariposa County Museum and History Center (located at 12th and Jessie streets). An outstanding interpretative center; carefully assembled displays transport visitors from native American beginnings, through Spanish California to the heydays of the Gold Rush itself. The grounds also display a complete *arrastra*, (mule powered apparatus popular among Mexican miners) and a recreation of a typical nineteenth century native American village.

At the California State Mining and Mineral Museum (located just south of town on the Mariposa County Fairgrounds) guests are treated to a walk through a mock mine tunnel and the sight of *real* gold; one of the world's largest nuggets in fact, weighing in at 13.8 pounds (mined in 1865, its value is estimated today at $80,000). Pick up a good practical knowledge and appreciation not only for the unique qualities of gold but for the unique nature of California as well as you wander amidst informative displays that explore and explain this State's and in particular Gold Country's unique and interesting geology.

In 1872, Levi received a letter that changed the course of the company's history, as well as the history of his famous pants. Jacob Davis, a tailor living in Nevada, had started placing metal rivets at the points of strain on the pants he was making for his customers. He regularly purchased bolts of cloth from Levi Strauss & Co., and in 1872 he wrote to the company, telling them about his invention and suggesting that they patent the process together. Levi was enthusiastic about the idea and the patent was granted on May 20, 1873.

They knew that demand would be great for the new-sturdier waist overalls, so Levi brought Jacob Davis to San Francisco to oversee the first West Coast manufacturing facility.

In 1890 - the year that the lot number 501 first appeared on the denim overalls - Levi and his nephews officially incorporated the company, though by this time the 61-year-old business man had begun to concentrate on other business and philanthropic pursuits.

In summing up Levi's life and the establishment of his business a San Francisco newspaper at the time of his death in 1902 wrote: "Fairness and integrity in his dealings with his Eastern factors and his customers and liberality toward his employees soon gave the house a standing second to none on the coasts...

"The great causes of education and charity have likewise suffered a signal loss in the death of Mr. Strauss, whose splendid endowments to the University of California will be an enduring testimonial of his worth as a liberal, public-minded citizen and whose numberless unostentatious acts of charity in which neither race nor creed were recognized, exemplified his broad and generous love for and sympathy with humanity."

JOAQUIN MURIETA

Without question the most famous and perhaps most misunderstood character to emerge from Gold Country's "Cavalcade of Stars" was Joaquin Murieta; the so-called Robin Hood of California.

Legend says that witnessing both his brother's lynching and the ravishing of his sweetheart by reprehensible miners eager to run Mexicans (Joaquin was actually by most accounts a Spanish Californian) off their claims, triggered Murieta's two-month rampage. Some twenty-nine murders and numerous accounts of thievery were subsequently attributed to the "outlaw".

In an era before mass communication the result of whatever "crimes" actually were committed by Joaquin were the report of incidents too numerous to account for taking place all across California and all attributed to the same Latin antihero. It would seem that the most heinous were in fact "copycat" incidents of a single act of revenge actually committed on the part of Murieta.

At the height of the publicity Joaquin, no doubt the inspiration for Hollywood's Zorro (the latter safely transplanted into the Spanish California of a decade earlier so as to avoid the racist overtones that created his real life persona) was in fact not thirty-five as reported but rather a mere nineteen years old; and did not travel with a band of well organized guerillas but actually rode alone or with a few friends.

As you will discover in most larger Gold Country communities, MARIPOSA's Chamber of Commerce offers an excellent self-guided walking tour map free of charge.

■——————◆——————■

To wander from Highway 49, is to discover for yourself even more Gold Rush treasure.

One such historical treat is the tiny village of HORNITOS northwest of and below MARIPOSA in the scruboak and, in summer and fall, tawny grasslands of the low country.

Spanish for "little ovens", the settlement most likely takes its name from the unusual adobe, oven-shaped graves found in a Mexican cemetery located here.

HORNITOS, in addition to being a distinctively Hispanic settlement, carries with it the reputation of having been one of the, shall we say "liveliest", camps in old California. The town itself was laid out around a central plaza or square, as is typical in Latin America. Its ruins today speak to us of the transition of a uniquely Latin territory as it merged in the cultural tidal wave that swept over all of Spanish California during the Gold Rush.

This was the "home" of the most famous of all Gold Rush era antiheroes; a Latin Robin Hood known as Joaquin Murieta. It was said that, like many of his Hispanic compatriots, Joaquin had come to the gold fields dedicated to work hard and make his fortune. As with many emigrants he suffered endless indignities at the hands of those who considered themselves and this land to be of and for "Americans". Ironically, by most accounts Joaquin was in fact a native-born Spanish Californian. The reality that Spanish California had only recently been acquired by the United States and that the roots of its Latin citizenry with their extended roots to Mexico ran deep; the land itself a legacy of a proud Spanish history, eluded many "American" prospectors altogether.

Before HORNITOS, neighboring QUARTZBURG was yielding great quantities of gold. Unscrupulous argonauts (as the forty-niners came to be called) from "the States" wanted the diggings to themselves and so, in a violent, lawless scene that was repeated all too often during the Gold Rush, "Mexican" miners were literally run out of town.

Murieta gained his reputation as California's Robin Hood following the imposition of a state-wide foreign miners tax; a political attempt aimed specifically at minorities in an attempt to keep them out of the gold fields. It was during this time when Hispanic argonauts were frequently unjustly accused of and punished for all sorts of crimes, including murder that young Joaquin took to his midnight raids in a spirited attempt to realign the offset balance of justice in "his country". An excellent horseman and a deadeye behind the trigger, he relished close calls, daring to rob "Americans" bent on "exterminating the Mexican race" in plain view of a pursuing posse and then somehow escaping "like a genie." Such bravado was well remembered by those who witnessed his flamboyance in ordering a bulletproof vest which he tested by shooting himself at point-blank range!

A reward was subsequently issued for the capture of Joaquin dead or alive. In one of the more gruesome chapters of Gold Rush history, bounty hunter Harry Love collected that reward when he delivered to state officials what he claimed to be the head of Murieta. Proudly displayed to the public in Sacramento, and later elsewhere, Joaquin undoubtedly enjoyed and regretted a most macabe twist of fate as all who knew him looked at the curly, sandy-haired, blue-eyed head on display (hardly the black-haired, brown-eyed Joaquin) and realized that not only had Love duped the State, but Joaquin had duped Love.

Regardless, from that grisly moment on, Murieta seems to have abandoned his escapades, perhaps content to know that he had made his point; distraught to have witnessed for himself how fighting violence with violence only precipitates more violence and in this case the murder of yet another innocent man.

Hence QUARTZBURG's sister-city HORNITOS was born. Being distinctly Hispanic, it became a refuge of sorts, albeit a rowdy one, for many a displaced Latino forty-niner. Lining the plaza today are anonymous buildings and/or mere foundations of the many saloons, fandango halls and gambling palaces of a disenfranchised population. A secret tunnel, clearly visible even today, just off the plaza itself, is said to have been the infamous Joaquin Murieta's escape route from his favorite fandango hall.

Also of particular note, just off "the square" are the remains of the first store ever owned and operated by Domingo Ghiradelli. Evidently HORNITOS and indeed all of old California had quite a sweet tooth, for Italian-born Domingo who supplied the town with chocolate confections brought with him via Peru, went on to become the now world-famous San Francisco chocolatier.

Much to the chagrin of QUARTZBURG "toughs" HORNITOS yielded abundant "color" not only culturally but from rich placers and quartz deposits of its own; becoming one of the most prosperous towns in the Mother Lode!

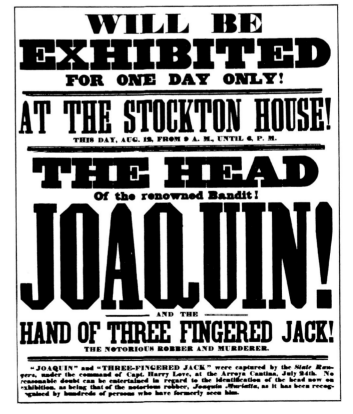

WILL BE EXHIBITED FOR ONE DAY ONLY!

AT THE STOCKTON HOUSE!

THIS DAY, AUG. 12, FROM 9 A. M., UNTIL 6, P. M.

THE HEAD

Of the renowned Bandit!

JOAQUIN!

AND THE

HAND OF THREE FINGERED JACK!

THE NOTORIOUS ROBBER AND MURDERER.

"JOAQUIN" and "THREE-FINGERED JACK" were captured by the State Rangers, under the command of Capt. Harry Love, at the Arroya Cantina, July 24th. No reasonable doubt can be entertained in regard to the identification of the head now on exhibition, as being that of the notorious robber, Joaquin Murietta, as it has been recognized by hundreds of persons who have formerly seen him.

QUARTZBURG "color" played out quickly and subsequently the town itself disappeared completely from the map.

————————◆————————

Just beyond the lawlessness that plagued the QUARTZBURG/HORNITOS area are the stately ruins of BEAR VALLEY; a rich center of "eastern" seaboard opulence and civility and the home of famed explorer-turned-statesman John Charles Fremont.

After purchasing, for $13,000, a vast "floating" Mexican land grant, Fremont allegedly floated the grant's boundaries to include this stretch of the Mother Lode once gold had been discovered on it.

In yet another of the many landgrabs that wrested from Spanish Californian aristocracy its birthright, the United States Supreme Court upheld Fremont's claim in 1859.

Tempers flared and tensions erupted into threatened violence when new arrivals, believing all of this "American" landscape to be open to their conquest, exercised "squatters rights", ignoring any land grant claims be they Mexican or American.

Those who took on the Captain, however, soon came to realize that they had challenged the wrong man. Recognizing that they in fact were holding "a grizzly bear by the tail", all eventually abandoned even the least questionable affront and left Fremont to his enterprise.

Grubstaking Mexican miners to work his newly acquired rich placers, Fremont went on to become the first to open a hardrock quartz mine in Gold Country. All produced handsomely in spite of his claim that expenses drained the income of his enterprise. Fremont sold the grant in 1863 for $6 million.

Little survives to speak to us today of the days when the Captain ruled his sizeable empire from "the residence" here. Nothing remains of the great house itself (which Fremont endearingly referred to as The White House), once staffed with French servants for his wife and children. Gone also is the splendid Oso House Hotel which Fremont had built to host visiting dignitaries such as the legendary journalist Horace Greeley and novelist Richard Henry Dana. But in the nearby town that took the name of the famed estate stand the famous Bon Ton Saloon (still in operation today as a restaurant), a boarding house,

DOMINGO GHIRARDELLI

Born in Italy in 1817, Domingo Ghirardelli was the son and apprentice of a celebrated chocolatier. Eager to strike out on his own, young Domingo journeyed to Peru when he was just 19 years old. There he established his own confectionery. While in Peru, he befriended an American cabinetmaker named James Lick, who, in 1847, moved to San Francisco carrying with him 600 pounds of Ghirardelli chocolate. Lick arrived in San Francisco in January 1848, exactly 13 days before the discovery of gold at Sutter's Mill.

Lured by Lick's tales of the gold rush, the adventurous Ghirardelli followed his friend to California in 1849. Upon arrival, he immediately set out for the gold country to seek his fortune. After a few discouraging months, he abandoned prospecting and opened a general store where he specialized in supplying chocolate to the burgeoning the Garbaromp Store, I.O.O.F. (International Order of Odd Fellows) Hall, which is today a museum and the Trabucco Store.

———◆———

To wander upslope off of Highway 49 from MARIPOSA is to ascend into the high country splendor of Yosemite by way of EL PORTAL.

Eight miles west of EL PORTAL one encounters a particularly interesting piece of history in the form of Savage's Trading Post.

Frontiersman James Savage (his name couldn't fit better if it had been conjured by a screenwriter on a faux western backlot in Hollywood), operated several such outposts in this then uncharted wilderness. He had found it more profitable to barter with the local native American population for gold than to get down into the dirt and dig it up for himself.

His trading posts turning enviable profits, James Savage, having befriended the indigenous community, according to legend, "took" a native bride or two.

Hostilities erupted when miners allegedly assaulted local Indian women. The mythically fierce Yosemites (Grizzly Bears) as forty-niners called them (actually these people referred to themselves as the Ahwahneechee or people of the valley of the tall grass) in retaliation attacked the one institution that symbolized a non-Indian presence; that being Savage's trading posts, burning them to the ground.

A fledgling state militia was mustered to track down and incarcerate the "offending" Indians. Savage was called upon to head up the task force. It was while in the process of so doing that he and his small band of soldiers became among the first to record, after stumbling upon, the grandeur of Yosemite Valley. So overwhelmed were they by the stunning vistas of veils of leaping waters suspended from sheer granite cliffs, magnificent Half Dome and monolithic El Captain that, according to one in the party, some of the men stood there with tears in their eyes; realizing that they were gazing upon what had to be one of the most sublime settings in all of the American west.

———◆———

population of miners. He stayed in Gold Country until 1852, when he moved to San Francisco.

Domingo's life and business survived low times as well as high times - from a devastating fire to near-bankruptcy to his revolutionary discovery of the Broma process in the 1860's (a special procedure still used to make one of Ghirardellis most popular products; sweet Ground Chocolate and Cocoa).

Domingo Ghirardelli died in 1894, leaving his legacy-Ghirardelli Chocolate, considered by many as one of the most outstanding chocolates produced in all the world.

By continuing to honor his European heritage of premium quality ingredients and slow, time-honored methods of manufacture, Ghirardelli remains as *the* premier American chocolate.

Photo by Ed Cooper

WHISTLING BILLY

"In Coulterville we begin to believe in the Gold Rush, for the town radiates history. It hangs thick in the air, like heat waves shimmering from the nearby dry gulches, where miners worked and cursed and sweated on hot August afternoons. History, here, is written in the sun baked adobe of the Sun Sun Wo Store, in the embossed tin walls of the Jeffrey Hotel and the silent gravestones on the hillside cemetery."
Don-Betty Martin: Travelwriter
team and Gold Country residents

orth from MARIPOSA, on Highway 49, after navigating a number of switchbacks descending past historic gold mines both open and closed, you arrive at COULTERVILLE; a gem of a Gold Rush town and a favorite among forty-niner aficionados. Redolent with antiquity and so unmarred by modern development, the entire town has been designated a state historic landmark; its main street listed on the National Registrar of Historic Places. No stone monument or signage is required to alert the traveler that he or she has stumbled upon a surviving relic of the Gold Rush.

Founded by George W. Coulter, who set up shop here in the spring of 1850; COULTERVILLE provided "possibles", as forty-niners were fond of calling "provisions", to an ever expanding population of fortuneseekers.

Following a pattern of growth typical among Gold Country "boomtowns", within five years the settlement had become transformed from a canvas "tent" city into a rough and tumble assortment of brick and adobe structures. In its heyday, COULTERVILLE (having established itself as a regional supply center), boasted dozens of general stores, ten hotels and 25 saloons!

Also typical of Gold Rush boomtowns, the entire settlement burned to the ground repeatedly. In the case of COULTERVILLE such conflagration occurred on three separate occasions (and oddly enough at 20-year intervals: 1859, 1879, and 1899). Each time the settlement reappeared like a phoenix from the flames, hastily thrown-up so as to keep pace with the gold seekers, who themselves kept on seemingly unaffected, in their frantic pursuit of treasure.

Three notable figures of the American west came to be linked with the once-bustling COULTERVILLE: Nelson Cody, brother of Buffalo Bill clerked and later managed a trading post housed in what subsequently became the Wells Fargo Building. At the nearby Jeffrey Hotel (still in operation) Ralph Waldo Emerson and President Theodore Roosevelt were said to have been guests (the latter reportedly while enroute to tour the Yosemite in 1909 with famed conservationist John Muir).

As mining dwindled COULTERVILLE too maintained its economic equilibrium as an important way station for travelers enroute to what became soon thereafter Yosemite National Park.

Sitting as it does, suspended both in time and geographic location, in a shallow upland valley where Highway 132 crosses Highway 49, COULTERVILLE affords travelers a pleasant look back. The Northern Mariposa County History Center, occupying portions of two of the towns most historic buildings (one of them being the aforementioned trading post/Wells Fargo Building), both

TM
Warner
Brothers

erected during the 1850's, serves as an excellent orientation center for visitors. Packed to overflowing with antiquities, the History Center is the perfect place from which to begin one's explorations. In front of the collection, under the "Hangman's Tree", sits "Whistling Billy". This steam engine from the nearby Mary Harrison Mine once pulled ore cars over four miles of track along "the crookedst railroad in the world."

To truly recapture the glory days of the Gold Rush, visit the Magnolia Saloon at the Hotel Jeffrey. Erected in 1851 as a fandango hall, its nearly 3-foot thick adobe walls insured its survival architecturally. Operators past and present have kept the breath-of-life flowing through its classic "batwing" doors, where today the cool, dark interior, wooden floor strewn with sawdust and "tinkling of the ivories" on the corner piano readily conjure up images of red-shirted, levi-clad forty-niners paying for their "poison" with gold dust pored from little leather pouches. Other notable surviving landmarks are the I.O.O.F. and Knights of Pythias halls.

At one time home to a large Chinese population, a charming Eastern relic, the Sun Sun Wo Store (still in operation) can be found among the scattered residences east of town. Standing adjacent to Sun Sun Wo you will discover yet another Gold Rush institution; that being the bordello (in this case Candy's Place). It is no longer in operation.

COULTERVILLE itself sustains a weathered look. Like a true "old-timer", it will share with you much about its past if you will slow yourself down from the rushed pace of modern-day life and listen.

———————◆———————

Northwest of COULTERVILLE, on highway 132, sits LAGRANGE. French for "barn", LAGRANGE was originally known as French Bar. Not surprisingly it was settled by French argonauts in 1852.

For a time, famed novelist Bret Harte taught school here and it is probably the setting for several of his most memorable short stories.

Today the entire town is listed on the National Register of Historic Places. Highlights to explore are the adobe museum, LAGRANGE jail and St. Louis Catholic Church. A large gold dredge is prominently displayed in the town's park.

———————◆———————

As you continue north on Highway 49 yet another twenty miles, traversing typical Mother Lode terrain with its intermittent stands of great oaks and sprawling grasslands (pine forests reaching down from the higher elevations); watch for tiny (formerly huge) CHINESE CAMP. At one time larger than San Francisco's Chinatown, descendants of these forty-niners no doubt *own* most of today's San Francisco Chinatown! Most notable here are the lovely locust-like "Trees of Heaven", originally imported together with the settlement's then indentured population, from China. These trees shade the stone walled ruins of a Wells Fargo Express office and iron door post office (both

SIERRA RAILWAY

dating back to 1854), and beautiful St. Francis Xavier Catholic Church (built in 1855).

The historic post office building today serves as an official Visitors Information Center for Tuolumne County, dispensing, along with other informative items, literature about the often downplayed contribution made by Chinese emigrants who after "working off" their indentured servant status went on to help build the West while facing incredible prejudice and personal indignations.

━━━━━◆━━━━━

Just beyond CHINESE CAMP and just off Highway 49 (along Highway 120), you stumble across KNIGHTS FERRY. Another Gold Rush relic its most notable glimmer survives in the form of a remarkable covered bridge (the longest such bridge in the United States) designed by Ullysus S. Grant and built in 1862 by the then president's brother-in-law.

Among the many Gold Rush era buildings still standing at KNIGHTS FERRY are The Dent house residence, an iron jail, the Masonic Hall, and the oldest continuously operated general store in California.

━━━━━◆━━━━━

> *"The whole country from San Francisco to Los Angeles and from the seashore to the Sierra Nevada resounds to the sordid cry of gold, gold! GOLD! While the field is left half planted, the house half built and everything neglected but the manufacture of shovels and pickaxes. . ."*
> —*The Californian, May 29, 1848*

old *still* makes the world go around at JAMESTOWN! As with COUTLERVILLE, JAMESTOWN readily conjures tangible visions of the Gold Rush itself. It too has seemingly never left the past. Once heralded as the gateway to the Mother Lode, a community-conscious citizenry continues making every effort to keep things that way.

Unlike COULTERVILLE, both placer and hardrock quartz mining continues on here; the town's brightly painted, two-story buildings filled with shopkeepers who'll readily pay you cash (at 20 percent below the going gold rate of approximately $400 an ounce) or turn your latest find into fine handcrafted jewelry for a nominal fee.

Still youthful and vibrant, Hollywood-savvy visitors will no doubt recognize familiar surroundings as JAMESTOWN, with its vintage Sierra Railroad (today a State Historic Park) has served as backdrop for everything from "Butch Cassidy and the Sundance Kid" and "High Noon" to "Finian's Rainbow" and "Back to the Future-Part 3".

One of Gold Country's earliest settlements, JAMESTOWN (locals call it Jimtown), was founded in 1848 by a lawyer, Col. George James, who became involved in an assortment of failed land schemes. James subsequently departed little more than a year later owing money to nearly every miner in the district. What had precipitated Mr. James arrival was the discovery of a 75 pound gold nugget at Woods Creek near present day Main Street!

Local fortuneseekers here often mine more from taking would-be prospectors out on a "washing gold" expeditions than from gathering in "color" themselves. Again, you won't begrudge a dollar spent for the opportunity of reliving the Gold Rush for yourself and for the very real chance of taking a bit of gold, personally discovered, home with you to help keep the memory. No one can express adequately to someone who has not been there what it is to feel one's heart thump at the first sight of raw gold! To experience that emotional sensation of "gold fever" is to define for any Gold Country explorer in unforgettable terms the very essence of California's Gold Rush. In JAMESTOWN weekend prospectors remain tight-lipped about tending to their claims.

While all of JAMESTOWN belongs in a history book, Main Street in particular, flaunts its Gold Rush heritage. The covered balcony architecture typical of the best preserved Gold Country towns is nowhere more boldly on display than here. Handsomely restored hotels, saloons and gold prospecting outfitters shops jostle for attention along a boardwalk straight out of a Hollywood western (and it is!).

Visitors won't want to miss nosing about town, visiting the historic Sierra Railway (open during summer months only) and perhaps trying their own hand at gold panning.

━━━━━◆━━━━━

During the 1850's SONORA and neighboring COLUMBIA competed intensely for preeminence. Today there is no question about which is the liveliest—SONORA, always the "biggest" and still booming, boasts one the busiest main streets to be found in the Mother Lode. As seat of Tuolumne County and a trading center for the surrounding cattle and lumber country, and as gateway to the Sierra Nevada foothills, this regional Gold Rush capitol continues to be the bustling community it has been for more than a century.

Originally settled early in 1848 and named after the Mexican State from which many forty-niners came, SONORA's early history was one plagued by ethnic contention and subsequent violence. Discrimination reached its peak in 1850 when a state-wide thirty dollar-a-month tax was levied on all "foreigners" intent on pursuing mining activities in California; legislation clearly motivated by bigotry and greed.

SONORA's population dwindled as Mexican miners departed enmasse, forced to abandon their claims, unable and/or unwilling to pay the offensive tax. Tensions heightened when French argonauts openly opposed the levied affront by proudly displaying French flags at each of their claims, leading to many an altercation with the boys from "the States". Local businesses suffered the most as an estimated 3,000 to 5,000 "customers" departed literally overnight.

California's rowdy but not altogether uncivilized populace rose up in revolt, repealing the offensive mandate the following year (in 1851). SONORA's displaced Mexican population together with the French, sensing that it was safe to return, did so and SONORA got on with the business of establishing itself as the most cosmopolitan center in the mines; in fact the Queen of the Southern Mines.

Washington Street of yesterday was lined (and still is) with buildings made haphazardly of adobe, hewn planks, sailcloth, and tin. Today contemporary facades cover aging structures. Yet even with its modern face, much of SONORA reflects the old days. A drive up and down the town's narrow, winding side streets reveals relics of a flamboyant past.

The Tuolumne County Historical Society Museum, housed in the century-old jail on West Bradford Street, showcases pioneer firearms, Tuolumne County's "official" gold collection and an informative display on westward migration as it occurred during the time of the Gold Rush proper. While visiting the museum, pick up a copy of a walking tour map of vintage homes and other points of historical interest (among them the impressive old cemetery on Yaney Street), free for the asking.

Unquestionably, the single most outstanding piece of architecture in SONORA is St. James Episcopal Church, which stands at the head of Washington Street (Highway 49) on the north end of town. Not the oldest building in this historic city, it is nevertheless the most elegant. It's Norwegian designer, the Reverend John G. Gassman, also served as the church's first pastor. Across the street from the church, the beautifully restored Street-Morgan Mansion today houses private offices. On the second floor of City Hall (94 West Washington Street) vintage fire fighting equipment, uniforms and other related memorabilia are handsomely displayed.

Other notable structures include the ubiquitous I.O.O.F. Hall, the stately County Building and the City Hotel. At the south end of town stands the Gunn House, SONORA's oldest residence. Built by Dr. Lewis C. Gunn in 1850 for his family, it later became the offices for the *Sonora Herald*, the first newspaper in the "southern mining district". Since remodeled, it is today operated as an inn.

The Big Bonanza Mine, believed to be the largest pocket mine ever discovered in the Mother Lode, was located on Piety Hill, less than one hundred yards from St. James Episcopal Church. First worked by Chileans, who discovered a large amount of surface gold, it was later purchased for a pittance in the 1870's by three partners. After several years of patient work, they broke through into a body of almost solid gold! Within one day they had sent $160,000 in 19th century dollars worth of gold to the San Francisco mint. Within a week another $500,000 had been extracted from the mine!

Remember to consider when evaluating the fortunes made that you are referring to the purchasing power of nineteenth-century dollars, and not that of the US dollar today. Also, it is important to remember that when referring to dollar amounts attached to gold strikes while touring Gold Country, that such numbers have most often been calculated to reflect the gold exchange rate as it stood in 1849 (which was then $16 an ounce) and not at the current gold exchange rate (which at the time of this printing stands at around $400 an ounce!).

———◆———

For a breathtaking sidebar to your Gold Country explorations, take Highway 108 as it soars from gold fields to evergreens to high Sierra grandeur. First you will pass through TUOLUMNE (with its charming collection of historic homes); then TWAIN HARTE (a modern and attractive community of summer homes). Beyond luxuriant alpine forests you climb to the heady heights of Sonora Pass, one of only four thoroughfares that actually breach (in season) the stupendous Sierra Nevada.

Gold Rush enthusiasts will find it difficult to resist descending into the eastern Sierra to visit such historic mining locales as BODIE (the State's finest example of a Gold Rush era ghost town).

————————◆————————

"How would you like to winter in such a abode? In a place where there are no newspapers, no churches, lectures, concerts or theaters; no fresh books, no shopping, calling nor gossiping little tea-drinkings; no parties, no balls, no picnics, no tableaux, no charades, no latest fashions, no daily mail (we have an express once a month), no promenades, no rides nor drives; no vegetables but potatoes and onions, no milk, no eggs, no nothing. I expect to be very happy here. This strange odd life, fascinates me."
-Dame Shirley- to her sister in Amherst, Massachusetts,
from a high Sierra mining camp, 1854.

 OLUMBIA has always held a special place in the heart of Californians. To the boys of forty-nine she was afforded the same reverence bestowed upon the rare sight of beholding a beautiful woman in the "camps". Proclaimed as the toast of the southern mines, COLUMBIA, with her red-brick face and wrought iron adornments was a showplace of the Mother Lode to be sure. Even today, her former glory days now long since faded, she remains as a mere "ghost town", still the grand dame of Gold Rush "cities".

With its unparalleled collection of restored buildings and outstanding displays of mining memorabilia, Columbia State Historic Park, situated two miles north and four miles off Highway 49, makes for a good starting point for anyone setting out to explore the Mother Lode. Today a community of "living history", for the best use of your time, stop by park headquarters for a brochure that outlines a self-guided walking tour. Information on historic buildings and sites within the "park" are keyed to this map of the town.

Gold was originally discovered here on March 27, 1850 by a Dr. Thaddeus Hildreth, placer mining in concert with associates. The camp was subsequently named Hildreth's Diggings, later American Camp, before being christened formally as COLUMBIA at the time of its incorporation back in 1852.

Its explosive beginnings astounded even Californians. At the time of its incorporation, less than two years after

BEAR AND BULL FIGHTS

During the Gold Rush, California's population was 95% male. Entertainment came in the form of fist fights, gambling, and dancing with one another ("ladies" wore arm bands for easy identification). Mexican miners introduced the traditional bull fight. Yankee enthusiasts, eager for greater action, created the spectacle of pitting a native California grizzly bear against the bull. Typical maneuvering of the bear was to grip the bull in a "bear-hug" and drag it down to the ground. The bull would, on the other hand, charge his assailant in an attempt to toss him up and gore him with his horns. This unique phenomenon gave rise to the Wall Street jargon of a bear (market is down) and bull (market is up) market.

Courtesy, Wells Fargo Bank

Photo by Mark Gibson

its founding, COLUMBIA had grown from a typical tent camp to a budding metropolis. No less than four banks, three express offices, eight hotels, a daguerreotype (photography) parlor, 17 general stores, two fire companies, 40 saloons, and fandango halls and gaming establishments too numerous to count all tempered by three churches, two bookstores, a temperance league and choral society COLUMBIA epitomized the exuberant, headlong *California enterprise* born out of the Gold Rush.

Irrepressible, this community never embarked upon an enterprise halfheartedly. When word reached "camp" that the first woman was about to arrive in town, the boys dropped their picks, shovels and pans, decorated Main Street with floral arches, mustered a brass band and marched down to SONORA several thousand strong to provide an "appropriate" escort.

Burned out a number of times, including one particularly disastrous blaze in 1854, the city was consequently rebuilt with brick, fireproof doors and iron shutters - one reason the state of COLUMBIA today is pretty much intact (restoration work continuing into the present).

Local area mines produced $87 million in gold! Many reminders of the expensive tastes this rich little city once afforded it's citizenry are still much in evidence, i.e. ornate black iron railing imported from Europe to use on upper-story balconies, the town's elegant and garishly decorated handpump fire engine (affectionately named Papeete), and a myriad of other surviving architectural extravagances.

COLUMBIA believed in culture. For entertainment she boasted three theaters, in which were showcased everything from Edwin Booth performing Shakespeare's Richard III to Lola Montez doing her infamous spider dance. The 1857 Fallon House Theater continues to feature year-round stage productions. Fallon House itself today also serves the community as an elegant hotel. Visitors are not encouraged to wander about the halls; but all are welcome to take a peek at the beautiful lobby and authentically furnished rooms, and of course to pay a visit to the Fallon House Ice Cream Parlor next door. Also serving overnight guests is the ornately furnished City Hotel (built in 1856).

At the William Cavalier Museum (housed in Sewell Kapp's Miners Supply Store), gain a quick perspective on the little city *the way it was.*

Children of all ages will enjoy panning for gold down in Matelot Gulch, riding the jouncing stagecoach from the Wells Fargo Express office (built in 1858) through the granite hills behind town, sipping sarsaparilla at a working "smithy", visiting the candy shop, or getting a haircut in the State's oldest barber shop. There's Hangtown Fry or some other forty-niner delicacy to sample amidst turn-of-the century elegance at Columbia House Restaurant.

St. Anne's Catholic Church, perched atop Kenebec Hill south of town overlooks the world's richest placer grounds. On a hill north of town stands a two-story brick schoolhouse built back in 1860. Behind the schoolhouse is Columbia's historic cemetery. Here, as elsewhere in Gold Country, the marble headstones are engraved with names of Spanish, French, Italian, and other extractions reflecting the truly worldwide influx of Gold Rush argonauts.

During the summer one can tour an operating quartz mine off Italian Bar Road. In addition, Columbia College, built around the San Diego Reservoir, encompasses a gigantic hydraulic mining basin. You'll pass the hydraulic mining monitor at Knickerbocker Flat on the way to the college.

Historically, COLUMBIA, during its heyday vied for positioning with SONORA as the largest town in the southern mines. Some fifteen thousand people lived here when the earth was yielding up a fortune in gold bullion. This city rang with the clamor of stagecoaches continually rattling into and out of town. Roads were crowded with freight wagons bringing in new provisions and merchandise from nearby STOCKTON.

Now, more than a century later, COLUMBIA is far removed from her glory days; and yet very much a "living" community.

———◆———

Just beyond COLUMBIA lies SPRINGFIELD. Named for a prodigious spring that once gushed forth from a granite out cropping as the source of Mormon Creek, forty-niners carted their gold-bearing "pay dirt" here for "washing". SPRINGFIELD was one of the best designed of all mining camps. There was, as with HORNITOS, a central plaza, from which the town spread out over a square mile.

The only building left standing on that Plaza today is the old brick Methodist Church which at one time also served (in addition to being a house of worship) as the settlement's school and courthouse.

———◆———

SHAWS FLAT was named for one Mandeville Shaw, who planted an orchard here in 1849. Of singular interest to the modern-day explorer is the Mississippi House (built in 1850 and still standing). It served this placer-mining settlement as a saloon, store and post office.

It was at a saloon that stood across the street from the Mississippi House that an enterprising bartender supplemented his daily wages in a particularly imaginative way. It seems that he would drop on the bar a bit of each pinch of dust that he took from the miners' "pokes" for their drinks. This took slight imagination; but the ingenious part of the larceny lay in his method of recovery.

Periodically leaving the bar to tramp around in the mud generated by a little spring behind the building, he would return to his station and carefully pick up, with his muddy boots, all the gold dust he had dropped and carefully brushed to the floor. At night he "panned out" the mud scraped from his boots to recover his rich "diggings". According to some accounts, the ingenious barkeep averaged about $300 a night during the week, and several times that on weekends!

SHAWS FLAT was the jumping off place in the career of James Fair who went on to amass a fortune on Nevada's Comstock Lode and is best remembered as the proprietor of San Francisco's Fairmont Hotel. There are many who say that it was he who tended bar at that now-vanished saloon across from the Mississippi House.

━━━━━━━━◆━━━━━━━━

Once a thriving placer-mining community along Mormon Creek, today TUTTLETOWN isn't much more than a wide spot along State Highway 49. You can still see the ruins of Swerer's Store, where Bret Harte was once a clerk and Mark Twain a customer.

In the midst of this once thriving mining region JACK-ASS HILL got its name from the braying of hundreds of mules that were tied up overnight when the pack trains stopped to rest.

The main attraction here today is a reconstructed cabin wherein Mark Twain lived for five months as the guest of William and James Gillis. It was while visiting here that Twain researched and wrote several of his most famous stories including a certain tale about a jumping frog in neighboring ANGELS CAMP.

Fourteen miles from Sonora, on State Highway 49, sits the village of CARSON HILL. Named for the hill that rises behind it, this hamlet, in its heyday, was

ARGONAUTS

considered to be the richest of the Mother Lode camps. The slopes of that hill yielded a fortune in gold bullion. A distinctive sign marks the precise spot where in 1848 California's largest recorded gold nugget was unearthed. It weighed 195 pounds and was worth about $43,000 (in those days). The consolidated mines of CARSON HILL and neighboring MELONES collectively produced over $26 million in gold!

CARSON HILL today has no buildings of any character left. The most conspicuous reminder of the mining days is what forty-niners referred to as the "glory hole" of the Morgan Mine in that famous hill above town. Fifteen miles of underground tunnels honeycomb the hill. One of the shafts reaches down almost five thousand feet (Gold Rush aficionados enjoy a visit to a fanciful recreation of this underground spectacle at world-famous Knotts Berry Farm in Southern California).

Mexicans who first established a camp on the banks of the Stanislaus River near the present crossing of State Highway 4 named it MELONES (Spanish for "melons") because the gold they found here resembled not melons (one can wish) but melon seeds. Later miners tried to change the name to Slumgullion in honor of the thick heavy mud which made mining in the area so difficult, but the original name clung even more tenaciously than the mud.

In 1848, John W. Robinson started the first ferry crossing in the area. It proved a profitable enterprise. During the summer of 1850 alone he had collected $10,000 (a tidy sum in those days) for ferrying freight, animals, and miners across the river. The story is told of a circus on its way to COLUMBIA whose owner tried to convince the operator to take their elephant, Lucy, across. Despite a heated argument, Robinson refused. Poor Lucy, attempting to swim, was carried downstream and subsequently drowned, whereupon the circus immediately disbanded (its cavalcade of performers, eager to mutiny anyway, promptly joining the ranks of the gold seekers).

Robinson's Ferry itself now lies beneath the waters of Melones Reservoir. Today only a plaque and a scenic viewpoint serve as reminders of this once colorful site.

MARK TWAIN

Born Samuel Langhorne Clemens, the American humorist, writer, newspaperman, and lecturer who won worldwide acclaim for his depictions of boyhood adventures on the Mississippi in fact began his prolific career as Mark Twain in Gold Country.

In 1861 Clemens headed west, where, after failing at prospecting, took up employment writing for Virginia City's Territorial Enterprise. Signing his work as Josh, he took great delight in perpetrating journalistic hoaxes such as the account of *The Petrified Man* and *Empire City Massacre*, so plausibly, albeit preposterous, that other newspapers reprinted the reports as being true!

Unable to give up the prospect of striking it rich, Twain took up mining again, this time at Angels Camp, where he heard the story that would make him famous. Published in New York as *The Celebrated Jumping Frog of Calaveras County*, the tale, artfully retold, was an immediate hit. The composite of his Gold Country adventures later appeared collectively in a tome entitled *Roughing It*.

From such beginnings Mark Twain went on to entertain with *The*

THE MOTHER LODE: NORTHERN DISTRICT

> *"Panning is a very curious and mysterious operation. I did as I was told, whirling and dipping with all my might. There was nothing in the appearance of the earth to distinguish it from what I had seen a thousand times at home. Yet this was the earth I had come twenty thousand miles to seek, and in that earth, there lurked, so I was told, grains of gold."*
>
> *Journal of a Forty-niner*

 NGELS CAMP takes its name from George Angel, a member of Col. Jonathan D. Stevensons Regiment of New York Volunteers who came West in 1848 to take part in the Mexican War. Disbanded in San Francisco, Angel founded a trading post at the junction of what would become known as Angels Camp Creek and Dry Creek. The town grew quickly during the 1850s, and, although the setting was somewhat altered by the pen, it was probably the town Bret Harte would write about in his legendary story *The Luck of Roaring Camp.*

Discovery of the quartz lode which was to make ANGELS CAMP one of the great mining centers in the Mother Lode is a story often retold by California historians and Gold Rush aficionados. A miner named Rasberry, for whom Rasberry Lane (still a public thoroughfare in ANGELS CAMP) was named, was having difficulty with his muzzle-loading rifle. The ramrod had jammed. In a moment of exasperation he accidentally fired his rifle into the ground. When he went to retrieve the displaced rod, he found a piece of rock which had shattered from the impact. It glittered with what was unmistakably gold! Rasberry took almost $10,000 from his new found claim in three days and went on to make a fortune following the vein thus discovered.

In fact it has been said that, with regards to discovering the location of gold ore, the forty-niner's best theory was to have no theory at all. Irregular distribution of the

Adventures of Tom Sawyer and *Huckleberry Finn*, deriving more gold from his talent than the Sierra foothills could provide.

BRET HARTE

Born Francis Bret Harte, by age 11 the U. S. writer who singularly created the Local-Colour School of American Fiction had his first verses published. In 1854 Harte traveled west to California where, after several years in Gold Country he achieved international acclaim upon the publication of *The Luck of Roaring Camp and Other Sketches.*

He hired Mark Twain while serving as editor of the "Californian" and collaborated with him on several plays.

Retiring to London after having experienced phenomenal success in America, Harte found a ready audience for his tales of California's Gold Country. His *Ingenue of the Sierras* and *A Protegee of Jack Hamblin's*, both published late in his career (in 1893) received great acclaim and proved to be as successful as his earlier works.

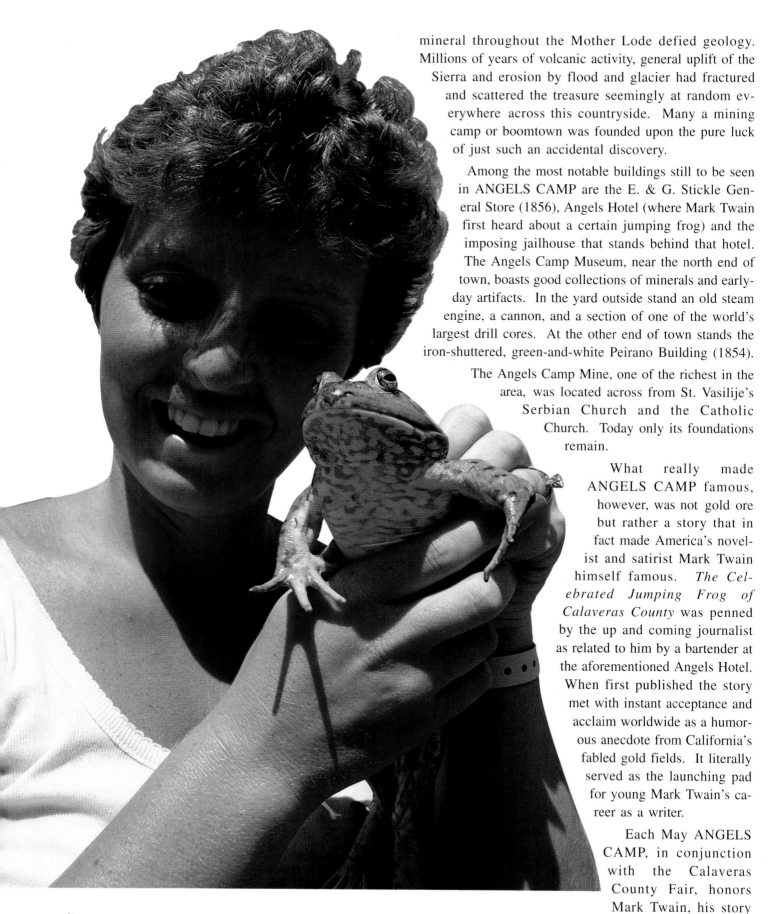

mineral throughout the Mother Lode defied geology. Millions of years of volcanic activity, general uplift of the Sierra and erosion by flood and glacier had fractured and scattered the treasure seemingly at random everywhere across this countryside. Many a mining camp or boomtown was founded upon the pure luck of just such an accidental discovery.

Among the most notable buildings still to be seen in ANGELS CAMP are the E. & G. Stickle General Store (1856), Angels Hotel (where Mark Twain first heard about a certain jumping frog) and the imposing jailhouse that stands behind that hotel. The Angels Camp Museum, near the north end of town, boasts good collections of minerals and early-day artifacts. In the yard outside stand an old steam engine, a cannon, and a section of one of the world's largest drill cores. At the other end of town stands the iron-shuttered, green-and-white Peirano Building (1854).

The Angels Camp Mine, one of the richest in the area, was located across from St. Vasilije's Serbian Church and the Catholic Church. Today only its foundations remain.

What really made ANGELS CAMP famous, however, was not gold ore but rather a story that in fact made America's novelist and satirist Mark Twain himself famous. *The Celebrated Jumping Frog of Calaveras County* was penned by the up and coming journalist as related to him by a bartender at the aforementioned Angels Hotel. When first published the story met with instant acceptance and acclaim worldwide as a humorous anecdote from California's fabled gold fields. It literally served as the launching pad for young Mark Twain's career as a writer.

Each May ANGELS CAMP, in conjunction with the Calaveras County Fair, honors Mark Twain, his story and Gold Rush days in general. The three-day event is climaxed by a jumping frog contest. The frogs give this fair its special quality. They arrive by the thousands. Some contestants bring them from distant and secret points. Others catch them in the marshy land adjacent to the fairgrounds itself. Any frog at least four inches in length from nose to base of tail is eligible to jump. Fame and riches go to the contestant whose frog achieves the greatest distance covered in three consecutive jumps. The strange and mystic rites performed by contestants to encourage their entries into Herculean efforts often overshadow the actual performance by the frogs themselves - the erratic behavior of human and frog adding up to what can only be described as a *very* entertaining show.

ANGELS CAMP has erected a monument to the frog along its main street and has placed an imposing statue of Mark Twain in its shady city park just off State Highway 49.

———◆———

East and upslope from ANGELS CAMP, on State Highway 4, sits VALLECITO (Spanish for "little valley"). First settled in 1850 by Mexican miners, it did not become a prominent camp until a rich strike in 1852. Still standing at the south end of town are the Dindelspiel Store (1851) and Wells Fargo Express office (1854). An old miner's bell and town monument are situated in front of the Union Church on Main Street. Two miles south of VALLECITO is Moaning Cave, a former Indian burial ground and one of three such caverns open to public inspection in Gold Country - (Mercer Caves and California Cavern being the other two).

A serene little community about two miles north of VALLECITO on State Highway 4, DOUGLAS FLAT has preserved only one stone-and-abode building from its mining days. The Gillead building (1851), with its two tall iron-shuttered doors, once served as both the town's general store and its bank. A safe inside was used as a vault for storing large quantities of gold. To be sure that it was adequately protected, an armed guard was stationed here at all times. The guard's "shotgun window" can be seen beside the rear door.

An interesting story is told about the Douglas Flat School. It is said that because the building was located on gold-bearing gravel, part of the teacher's contract included the right to pan for gold during recess!

———◆———

"Gold fever was as contagious as the itch. If ya took it, brimstone and grease would not cure you. The only remedy was for ya to go to the mines and try yer luck."
Journal of an Anonymous Argonaut, 1850

all Chinese Trees of Heaven form an inviting canopy over the streets of the grand old town of MURPHYS. In their shade, life goes on much as it has through the decades since the Gold Rush subsided.

MURPHYS is one of the most charming towns in the Mother Lode. It is an ideal place to relax and "soak up" some Gold Country atmosphere, sitting as it does in the heart of Gold Country's wine country, while enjoying fine dining and fine wine at, say, the historic Murphys Hotel. Top it all off with a memorable evening stroll through this, one of the best-preserved Gold Rush towns in California.

First settled in July of 1848 by brothers John and Daniel Murphy, its rich diggings built the substantial town of brick and limestone buildings that one sees today.

Most prominent among these old structures is the famous Murphys Hotel. It was erected by James Sperry and John Perry in 1856 as appropriately the Sperry and Perry Hotel, to accommodate the growing number of visitors passing through on their way to view the recently discovered giant sequoias or Sierra redwoods. To examine the old register is to find names of such illustrious "tourists" as Mark Twain, Ulysses S. Grant, Henry Ward Beecher, Thomas Lipton, J. Pierpont Morgan, Horatio Algiers, and one "Old Dan the Guide" from "God knows where". You will also find the entry of one "Charles Bolton, Silver Mountain". No one would have suspected this refined gentleman to be the notorious stage robber, Black Bart!

Across the street from Murphys Hotel is the Segale building (erected in 1856). It served as a bakery and miners' supply store.

Also built in 1856, the Peter L. Traver building is the oldest structure in MURPHYS, having survived all three fires that swept through the former mining camp. It now houses the Old Timers Museum. A pioneer blacksmith shop stands behind the building. The I.O.O.F. Hall and the Carley and Compere Buildings (all dating back to the 1850s) are among other notable vintage structures adjacent. Murphys Elementary School, which was built in 1860, is the oldest continuously-operated elementary schoolhouse in California. The Putney-Sperry house (built around 1857) off the Main Street at 518 Church Street, is a fine example of an early Gold Country Victorian residence.

North of town, on Sheep Ranch Road, St. Patrick's Catholic Church (built in 1858), is considered to best reflect early Gold Country construction techniques. Financed and built by the miners, clay used in the bricks was taken from nearby hills.

———◆———

Large stands of Sequioandendron Giganteum, (giant sequoias) about 20 miles northeast of MURPHYS on State Highway 4 at Calaveras Big Trees State Park are a must see. They were reported by John Bidwell who "discovered" them while he was on a scouting expedition in 1841. However, credit for announcing their existence to the world is usually given to A. T. Dowd, a hunter from MURPHYS, who brought the prehistoric dendroids to public attention in 1852. Today Calaveras Big Trees State Park offers an extraordinary setting for an invigorating morning walk. Camping, picnicking, and hiking, as well as swimming

and fishing in the North Fork of the Stanislaus River are also popular activities here.

———◆———

A little further upslope is the tiny mountain hamlet of SHEEPRANCH. George Hearst, later United States Senator from California and father of newspaper tycoon William Randolph Hearst, ran the Sheepranch Quartz Mine (which consequently helped launch the vast Hearst family fortunes). Legend maintains that this particular hardrock mine was a profitmaker from the time the first shovelful was dug!

———◆———

MOUNTAIN RANCH was the site of an early sawmill. Three or four Gold Rush Era buildings remain standing here today. Among them Domenghini's General Store is the most ancient structure in town. The stone edifice across the street from the store, a former fandango hall, now respectably houses a collection of Gold Rush memorabilia.

———◆———

At the northern junction of state Highways 4 and 49 at what was first known as Forks in the Road, today's

MINER'S TEN COMMANDMENTS

Miners were forced to write their own laws which gradually spread throughout the camps and became known as the Miner's Ten Commandments:

1. Thou shalt have no other claim than one.
2. Thou shalt not make any false claim nor jump one. If thou do thou must go prospecting and shall hire thy body out to make thy board and save thy bacon.
3. Thou shalt not go prospecting before thy claim gives out. Neither shall thou take thy gold to the gambling table in vain.
4. Thou shalt remember the Sabbath. Six days thou mayest dig, for in six days labor thou canst work enough to wear out thy body in two years.
5. Thou shalt not think more of thy gold than how thou shall enjoy it.
6. Thou shalt not kill thy body by working in the rain. Neither shall thou destroy thyself by getting "tight" nor "high seas over" while drinking down thy purse.

7. Thou shalt not grow discouraged, nor think of going home before thou hast made thy pile.
8. Thou shalt not steal a pick, a shovel or a pan from thy fellow miners, nor borrow a claim, nor pan out gold from others riffle box. They will hang thee, or brand thee like a horse thief with the letter R upon thy cheek.
9. Thou shalt not tell any false tales about "good diggings" in the mountains, lest your neighbors return with naught but a rifle and present thee with its contents thereof and thou shall fall down and die.
10. Thou shall not commit unsuitable matrimony nor neglect thy first love. If thy heart be free thou shall "pop the question" like a man, lest another more manly than thou art should step in before thee, and then your lot be that of a poor, despised comfortless bachelor.

ALTAVILLE was settled back in 1852. A lively little burg during the short period when placer mining held out, there are still today a few buildings worth noting. First is the handsome Prince and Garibardi Store, a well-preserved, two-story stone building erected in 1857 and still in use today. Close by is the oldest iron foundry in California, originally established in 1854 to repair mining machinery and to manufacture simple tools.

Also of note is another of the State's first schools. It can be found on the State Division of Forestry's grounds near ALTAVILLE. This red brick building was erected in 1858 and served the community until 1950.

━━━━━━◆━━━━━━

South and downslope from ANGELS CAMP along Highway 4 sits COPPEROPOLIS. As its name implies, COPPEROPOLIS was one of the few towns in Gold Country whose fortunes were tied to a mineral other than gold. One of the principal copper-producing centers in the United States during the Civil War, it boasted a population of several thousand people from 1860 to 1867, during which time it produced ore at an astonishing rate.

Strangely enough, the ore extracted was not smelted anywhere near the mines themselves. Rather, it was carried by cart to STOCKTON, then by river boat to SAN FRANCISCO, and finally by sailing ship around Cape Horn to New England and Swansea, Wales, for processing! Forty-niners often found themselves in the same circuitous but strangely efficient set of circumstances as they frequently sent their laundry out to Hawaii (it making the rounds and returning promptly cleaned and pressed [fluff and fold] in about a months time)!

Some of the old buildings in COPPEROPOLIS were built during the 1860s of brick hauled from nearby CO-LUMBIA (where "perfectly good stores" were being torn down by miners to get at the gold-rich soil underneath their foundations). At the south end of town are three such notable structures. The largest - a building with huge iron shutters and doors - was once the Federal Armory and served as headquarters for the Copperopolis blues during the Civil War. Next door are the old warehouse and office buildings of the Copper Consolidated Mining Company. The headframes and waste dumps of the mining operations can be seen across the street. At the other end of town is the I.O.O.F. Hall (originally a church and more recently a community center).

Behind COPPEROPOLIS lies the site of a famous Mother Lode town that never actually existed. While Mark Twain was busy commencing to write his famous frog story back at ANGELS CAMP, Bret Harte was committing to copy his classic *The Outcasts of Poker Flat*. Hartes POKER FLAT was set in this valley (then known as O'BRYNES FERRY and since inundated behind Turlock Dam).

Highway 4 continues on roughly parallel to Highway 49, traversing the picturesque former Mother Lode camp of CALAVERITAS. The only Gold Rush era survivor here is Luigi Costas store; an adobe structure built in 1852.

"I've labored long for bread
For honor and for riches,
But on my corns too long you've tread
You fine haired Sons of Bitches."

Note left behind for Wells Fargo
and signed by Black Bart, the Po8

eanwhile, back on highway 49, new roadways and other demands of modern civilization have stripped SAN ANDREAS of much of its mining camp character. Nevertheless left behind are a few classic Gold Rush structures. These remnants include the dressed-stone Fricot Building (which now houses the county library and Chamber of Commerce), a two-story I.O.O.F. Hall and Masonic Temple (both built in 1856), and the Courthouse (1867), today home of Calaveras County and an informative museum. Behind the courthouse is the old jail with a cell marked prominently "Black Bart slept here".

Black Bart's involvement with SAN ANDREAS was brief but profound. It has been calculated that between 1877 and 1883 he single-handedly held up 28 stage coaches. Wearing a flour sack for a mask, brandishing an empty shotgun and always polite to the passengers, throughout his "career" as a highwayman he never fired a shot.

The fact that on at least two occasions he left his victims with a bit of verse, poetry of his own creation, assured him a place in California lore. The fact that his first and last holdup took place just outside of SAN ANDREAS (at nearby Funk Hill) aligned his name forever with the history of that town.

A huge cement plant south of the city today employs many SAN ANDREAS residents. A century ago, these same rich gravels yielded gold to the Hispanic miners who first settled the town back in 1849, then to Americans who crowded them out in 1850, and finally to thousands of Chinese who had the patience to rework the tailings then considered "played out" and useless by others.

◆

Just to the east of State Highway 49 north of SAN ANDREAS sits that city's forever rival. MOKELUMNE HILL's historic prominence eludes Gold Country outsiders today. Infamous for a spell during the 1850's when a murder occurred at least once a week and an all out battle (in which many were killed) annually, MOK HILL, as

BLACK BART

Charles Boles (also known as Charles E. Bolton), was a refined gentleman, a gifted poet and a formidable long-distance walker. This latter ability came in handy as Charles Boles was also an accomplished outlaw who literally walked to and from (no matter how remote), the scene of the crime.

Under his chosen alias of Black Bart, between the years 1877 and 1883 he perpetrated twenty-eight robberies (all against the Wells Fargo Express Company). Yet he is remembered equally in San Francisco for his elegant life-style and love of the finer things. It was his success as a highwayman and not as a miner, that supported his *bon vivant* status.

Often walking as much as thirty miles in a single day, typically he faced down his selected victim by standing directly in front of an approaching stage coach as it rounded a corner in a most out-of-the-way backcountry heist. Wearing a long coat, and a flour sack with eye holes cut out, pulled over his head and brandishing a fire arm aimed directly at the driver, Boles would order him locals call it, today paints a far different picture of itself. Loosing the county seat (which it had held from 1852 until 1866) to SAN ANDREAS set its fate to languish. Yet it is because of such circumstances that MOKELUMNE HILL today stands as one of the Mother Lode's more picturesque towns. Quiet streets, a good collection of period architecture and distinctive mountain ambiance combine to make MOK HILL an enjoyable place to relax, study and explore.

Many of the structures here are built of a light brown stone known as rhyolite tuff (a material common to much of the Mother Lode). Best known reminders of the Gold Rush are the I.O.O.F. Hall (built in 1854 and the first three-story building ever to be erected in Gold Country), the remains of the L. Mayer and Son Store (1854), McFadden's Store (1854), the "Italian" Store (1854), the Wells Fargo Building (1865) and the beautiful wooden Congregational Church (built in 1856). The famous Hotel Leger (still operating today as an inn) embraces the building that once served as county courthouse. When the county seat was moved to SAN ANDREAS, George W. Leger simply incorporated the abandoned seat of government into his adjoining hotel.

Gold was first discovered here in 1848 by discharged members of Stevenson's regiment (see ANGEL'S CAMP). MOKELUMNE HILL began when hungry miners requisitioned an entrepreneur by the name of Syree to establish a supply depot for the nearby diggings.

The "diggins" here were so rich that in certain areas claims were limited to 16 square feet!

---◆---

> "When I got there
> The mining ground was staked and claimed.
> For miles around."
> A favorite gold camp song

 Mother Lode town that has kept pace with the times, JACKSON today is a modern community. City planners strive to preserve their Gold Rush heritage while attending to the demands of twentieth-century commerce. The community had its beginnings as a provisioning station at the point where the Carson Pass Emigrant Trail over the high Sierra met up with roads from SACRAMENTO and STOCKTON.

---

to, "Please throw down your strong box!" which he would then open with a hatchet. In all of his infamous career he never fired a shot (possibly never even loaded his firearm). It was his commanding presence and bravado, as well as the fact that he often rigged up sticks to make it appear as if he had a gang of armed comrades in tow, that caused those tough frontier stage coach drivers to obey.

Returning to the scene of his first holdup just outside Copperopolis, Boles was wounded slightly. The "gentleman" dropped his handkerchief which bore a Chinese laundry mark traced back to San Francisco by special law enforcement agent Harry Morse.

Confessing only to this, his *last* crime, Boles was sentenced to six years in San Quentin. Released for good behavior after having served only four, Charles E. Bolton *disappeared* forever; reportedly living off of a monthly allowance paid to him by Wells Fargo officials in exchange for *not* stealing their gold shipments.

> *Here I lay me down to sleep,*
> *To wait the coming morrow.*
> *Perhaps success, perhaps defeat,*
> *And everlasting sorrow.*
> *Let come what will I'll try it on,*
> *My condition can't be worse;*
> *And if there's money in that box*
> *Tis munny in my purse.*
> *Black Bart, the Po8.*

One of Stephen Foster's earliest songs became a favorite with the forty-niners. With a few subtle alterations made, the "theme song" of the California Gold Rush was:

I came from Alabama
    With my banjo on my knee,
I'm going to California
    My true love for to see.
It rained all night
    The day I left,
The weather it was dry,
    The sun so hot
I froze to death,
    Susanna, don't you cry!

Oh, Susanna!
Oh, don't you cry for me!
For I'm going to California
With my banjo on my knee.
-Stephen Foster

Oh California!
That's the place for me
I'm off to Sacramento
With a wash bowl on my knee!

OH, SUSANNA!

Gold being the most important element in JACKSON's economy for many decades, its fortunes were sustained not by placer mining but by the large hardrock quartz mines surrounding the area. Two of the most important were the Argonaut and Kennedy mines, both north of town and located across the highway from each other. Each had some of the deepest vertical shafts in the world (extending well over 5,000 feet into the ground) and each played significant roles in the economic development of the State, long after most other mines had been abandoned.

The Kennedy Mine started in 1856 and operated sporadically until 1942, producing $50 million in gold ore. Its most famous features are the huge tailing wheels which were built in 1912 to carry waste gravels away from the mine. They can be seen from State Highway 49 and without a doubt are "the most photographed, etched, sketched and painted mining item in the Mother Lode". One can walk up for a closer view by driving out Jackson Gate Road and taking a well-marked trail. Only two of the giant "wheels" remain standing in their original positions. The others lie in ruins - victims of age and the elements (plans are underway for their restoration).

The Argonaut, easily recognizable today by its lofty water tank, commenced operation in 1850. It produced continuously between 1893 and 1942 yielding $25 million in gold ore. The Argonaut also became infamous as sight of the worst mining disaster ever recorded in the Mother Lode. It happened in 1922 when forty-seven men became trapped by fire in the mine. Frantic rescue operations lasted for three weeks as volunteers dug connecting tunnels from the Kennedy Mine in an attempt to rescue the trapped miners. When the miners inside were located, all were dead. A carbide lamp had been used to write a grisly epitaph; "Gas too strong - 3 a.m."

Centerpiece in historic JACKSON today is the National Hotel's Louisiana House. Built in 1849 and since "restored" it is still open for lodging and dining.

JACKSON's Amador County courthouse, also still standing, opened in 1854 amid much pomp and circumstance. Regal ceremonies, including marching band and contingents of civil servants rapidly grew out of hand when local saloon keepers, caught up in the civic pride of the moment, offered free drinks all around. The wild "block-party" that ensued is remembered as having been legendary.

One of the more interesting buildings in JACKSON is the Historic Brown house. Built in the 1860s on a hill about two blocks east of downtown, it now serves as the Amador County Museum (where you can watch scale-models of the Kennedy and Argonaut mines in operation).

As elsewhere in Gold Country, many of JACKSON'S original structures were razed in conflagration (this blaze occurred in 1867). The Amador County Chamber of Commerce publishes a complete guide to *all* historic sites in JACKSON; pointing out both landmarks still standing as well as those identified today only with plaques. A good place to pick up a copy is here at the museum (225 Church Street).

Elsewhere, on narrow Main Street, stands the obligatory I.O.O.F. Hall. At Pioneer Hall the Order of Native Daughters of the Golden West was organized on September 11, 1886. Nearby, St. Sava's Serbian Orthodox church, built in 1894, is unusual for its architectural style. This small structure is the mother church for today's entire North American flock of faithful.

At Jackson Elementary School (intersection of Church and North Streets) an historical marker commemorates this site as the location of the first synagogue in the Mother Lode. Nothing remains today of that pioneer religious structure.

◆

Twelve miles northeast of JACKSON State Highway 88 climbs from oak woodlands up onto the "volcano" and into the bracingly pine-scented timberbelt.

Like MOKELUMNE HILL, but smaller, VOLCANO is one of those charming Gold Rush era towns that isn't re-stored, but rather, simply survived abandonment of the placers and the hydraulic mining that gave birth to it. As one historian so aptly put it, "Volcano is still Volcano, though its erupting days are over."

Its unusual location, in a high, mountain-rimmed basin where members of Stevenson's New York Eighth Regiment of Mexican War Volunteers witnessing the morning mist rising from that basin fancied it to *be* a volcano, keeps this settlement seemingly locked away from the world of 20th Century California.

Gold was first discovered here in 1848 by members of the regiment. The first mining camp grew quickly into a city of 5,000 miners. It formed the center of a rich placer mining area that produced some $90 million in gold! When the placer workings gave out, hydraulic mining tore the

JACKSON TAILING WHEELS

We're sons of gallant fathers, boys,
And mothers kind and true,
Who whispered as they wrung our hands
"God bless and be with you".
Wives, scores of sympathizing friends,
Who wish us hearty speed,
Besides the world back us, if
Our steps to fortune lead.

Chorus: Oh California!
Thou land of glittering dreams
Where the yellow dust and diamonds, boys,
Are found in all thy streams!

And all of us—have we not left
Our best of life for this!
But cheer we up! We will return
Laden with gold and bliss!
Then saddle our mules! Away we go
With hopes by fancy led,
To where the Sacramento flows
Over its glittering bed!

*A popular song sung to the
tune of Oh Susanna!*

GALLANT SONS

soil away from the limestone bedrock and sent it funneling through sluices.

To best explore the town's fine collection of Gold Rush era buildings one but needs to stroll its streets. The few surviving stone buildings dispense information of local history as well as Gold Country souvenirs. The town's most imposing structure, the three-story balconied St. George Hotel (built in 1862), is still open for business.

Other notable structures lining Main Street include the Kelley & Sigmond Building (1855), the iron-shuttered Clute Building (1855) and Meyer's cigar store (1856). Nearby Charleston Road's heirlooms include the Sing Kee Store (1854) and I.O.O.F. Hall and Masonic Temple (both built in 1856).

VOLCANO claims many "firsts" in California's cultural development: first public library, first literary and debating society, first astronomical observatory, first "little theatre" movement. It also had its fair share of saloons and fandango halls with which to fill the miners' idle hours with other less praiseworthy past times. At one time there were three breweries and three dozen saloons in this little town. One of the crumbling stone buildings still stand-ing on the west side of main street housed *two* separately-operated bars.

Perhaps the most unusual reminder of Volcano's past is "Old Abe," the Gold Country cannon that helped to win the Civil War. VOLCANO's Union volunteers wheeled out "Old Abe" to put down a threatened Confederate uprising. Control of VOLCANO might have meant that the area's gold would be diverted to the Southern cause. The story is told that in the absence of iron cannon balls, Union defenders gathered round, river-smoothed stones to use as ammunitions. "Old Abe" won the battle without firing a shot, its mere presence squelching any thought of an uprising.

Just south of town on the Volcano-Pine Grove Road, are limestone caves where the area's first Masons once held their meetings. These caves are well marked and open to public viewing.

Three miles northeast of VOLCANO is Daffodil Hill, famous for its acres of bulbs (all in full bloom during the early part of spring) and fascinating Indian Grinding Rocks State Park (literally a native American mess hall that pre-dates historic times).

> *"Most forty-niners were young men. Seldom called by their real names, they answered to sobriquets like Sailor Jack, Fuzzy, Red Rover, Dutch Jake and Pious Pete. It was not always healthy or polite to inquire too closely into a man's background unless he volunteered it. A popular ditty in the gold fields was:*
>
>> *Oh, what was your name in the States?*
>> *Was it Thompson, or Johnson or Bates?*
>> *Did you flee for your life,*
>> *Or murder your wife?*
>> *Say, what was your name in the States?*

utter Creek was named for Captain John Sutter, who himself attempted prospecting here. It is in fact one of the great ironies of the California Gold Rush that one of the wealthiest men in California, whose enterprise precipitated the discovery of gold and subsequent rush to the gold fields, was in fact left behind in ruins by it; his loosely held empire collapsing all about him as hired hands abandoned their tasks to become fortune seekers in their own right and emigrants invading, staking out and claiming "squatter's rights" to his lands. Sutter died in Washington D.C. fighting to the end for the federal government to restore and/or reimburse him for the empire wrested from his hands by unknowing or indifferent fortune seekers.

Ever unsuccessful at mining, John Sutter, in yet another ironic, if not brutal twist of fate, left SUTTER CREEK only to have the gold beneath his feet discovered and unearthed shortly thereafter in the early 1850s. That gold produced a fine crop of millionaires; among them was one Leland Stanford.

Stanford, who ran a drygoods store, acquired a share of Sutter Creek's Lincoln Mine as payment for one of his customer's debts. He worked the mine himself for months with no success. Discouraged and on the verge of selling off his share, he was convinced by Robert Downs, his foremen, to hang tough and not abandon the enterprise. Downs admonitions and Stanford's dedication paid off big when shortly thereafter they struck a vein of gold that yielded millions of dollars worth of gold bullion.

Stanford, of course, went on to become one of California's wealthiest citizens when he, together with Collis P. Huntington, Mark Hopkins and Charles Crocker invested their fortunes as the Big Four Railroad Barons.

SEEING THE ELEPHANT

The phrase "seeing the elephant" came to mean the excitement of the lure of California gold. It is said to have originated in a story about a farmer who had heard of elephants but had never seen one.

When a circus came to a nearby town, he loaded his wagon with eggs and vegetables and started for the market, determined to see a circus elephant. On the way he met the circus parade, led by the elephant.

The farmer was enchanted, but his horses were terrified. They bucked, pitched, overturned the wagon and ran away, scattering eggs and bruised vegetables over the countryside.

"I don't give a hang," said the farmer, "I have seen the elephant!"

He later became state senator, then governor and ultimately founder of one of America's great universities.

Sutter Creek's Central Eureka Mine, whose tailings can still be seen at the south end of town, proved to be yet another of the richest gold mines in all of California. It also came to be one of the most long-lived, operating up until 1958.

Awash in such wealth SUTTER CREEK proceeded to line its streets with handsome homes, many of which still stand. The SUTTER CREEK of today is by all accounts the most "charming" town in Gold Country, both from a visual standpoint as well as from a shopper's eye. This most attractive collection of Gold Rush architecture (its downtown business district contending with that of NEVADA CITY's historic Broad Street for preeminence as "most appealing thoroughfare" in Gold Country) packs into its four-block-long business district a remarkable and memorable collection of shops and shopkeepers.

Tin-roofed stores of yellow pine clapboard, brick and rough-hewn stone all juxtapositioned along a raised wooden sidewalk (built so pedestrians could avoid the muddy, unpaved streets of the 19th century) harbor a trea-sure-trove of history: the Masonic and I.O.O.F. halls (1869), Methodist Church (1862), stone Bartolo Brignole General Store (1859), and Belotti Inn (1860), the Leraggio Opera House (1860); to name but a few!

SUTTER CREEK is also home to the State's oldest continuously-operated water-powered foundry and machine shop; Knight Foundry (81 Eureka Street). Built in 1873 to supply machinery for the area's hardrock mining industry, today it offers guided tours pointing out the many innovations designed here and subsequently used throughout the West in the days before the introduction of electricity.

Visitor information and walking tour maps are available at the city clerks office in the civic auditorium located just south of the business district on Highway 49 where it crosses Sutter Creek.

◆

Smaller than SUTTER CREEK, but equally charming is neighboring AMADOR CITY (named for local ranchero Jose Maria Amador). The first quartz discovery in what is today Amador County was made here by a Baptist preacher. Because of this association the strike was known

In a cavern, in a canyon,
Excavating for a mine,
Dwelt a miner, forty-niner,
And his daughter, Clementine.

Light she was and like a fairy,
And her shoes were number nine,
Herring boxes without topses,
Sandals were for Clementine.

Drove she ducklings to the water,
Ev'ry morning just at nine,
Hit her foot against a splinter,
Fell into the foaming brine.

Ruby lips above the water,
Blowing bubbles soft and fine,
But alas, I was no swimmer,
So I lost my Clementine.

Then the miner, forty-niner,
Soon began to peak and pine,
Thought he oughter join his daughter,
Now he's with his Clementine.

In my dreams she still doth haunt me,
Robed in garments soaked in brine;
Though in life I used to hug her,
Now she's dead I draw the line.

**Oh, my darling, Oh, my darling,
Oh, my darling Clementine!
You are lost and gone forever,
Dreadful sorry, Clementine!**

CLEMENTINE

as "Ministers' Claim". Hardrock quartz mining provided the economic base for AMADOR CITY. The headframe of the very rich Keystone Mine can be seen on the eastern slope above the south end of town. The Mine House is located in the original Keystone Consolidated Mining Company's brick buildings and today operates as an inn.

State Highway 49 passes through the middle of AMADOR CITY, known for being the smallest incorporated city in California. You'll have no trouble locating the town's historic Imperial Hotel and the aforementioned Mine House Inn (both built back in the 1850s).

Highway 49 then swings through DRY TOWN. Founded in 1848, it is the oldest community in Amador County. Contrary to its name, the town actually supported twenty-six saloons in its heyday. In fact nearby Dry Creek, not abstinence, was the source of the town's name. The placer diggings here gave out in 1857, after which a fire leveled most of that which remained of the settlement. Several brick buildings, dating from 1851, survived that blaze. They still stand alongside the highway. Principal among them is a prominent brick store believed

to have been the mine office of legendary empire builder George Hearst.

Passersby get only a fleeting glimpse up the hill at DRYTOWN's historic cemetery. There is no public access. The interesting tombstones here date back to the early 1850s.

About a block east of Claypipers Theatre, Highway 49 passes an adobe-and-rock house, one of Amador County's oldest homes. Though the exact date of its construction has not been pinpointed, it was in fact erected prior to the Gold Rush.

———————◆———————

Beyond the near ghost towns of PLYMOUTH and LATROBE, sits FIDDLETOWN; a sleepy, tree-shaded village in the center of a prosperous dry farming belt, still worked in many cases by descendants of the pioneers who first settled here during the 1850s.

The flavor of FIDDLETOWN'S glory days is today preserved by a few fine surviving structures; all of which can be found grouped within a couple of blocks of each other. Of particular note is the Chew Kee herb doctor's

GOLD!

Formed in antiquity, within the earth's molten core, gold is a mixture of liquids and gases which, in solution with silica, make their way towards the outer surface of the planet. With a uniquely low melting point, (1,063 degrees Celsius), when compared to that of other metals, gold often, when heated by volcanic activity, liquefies, cools and redistributes itself in veins or pockets. Quartz is a common host for such "deposits".

Because of its composition the earliest of artisans found gold to be not only beautiful but malleable; easily forging it into works of art and adornment.

Virtually corrosion free, gold coins found in sunken Spanish galleons, after centuries of exposure to salt water, still glitter. Such qualities, making it in the eyes of mankind a sensuous, seemingly indestructible, in fact "eternal" element preferred over all else. Gold became the stuff of which dreams were made, the key to security and power, a *constant* either as bullion or art in a world of constant change.

Inscriptions in Egyptian tombs as early as 3500 B.C. reveal panning techniques for placer mining similar to those employed by forty-niners having been used for "washing gold" more than 50 centuries ago. With slaves to do the mining, Egyptian royalty amassed perhaps as much as five million pounds of *eternal* gold (the crypt of child king Tutankhamen among its treasures including a 242-pound golden coffin in which to transport the pharaoh to eternity).

Both the Greeks and Romans accumulated vast quantities of gold, mostly through conquest.

California's motherland, Spain, too possessed large quantities of gold which Roman conquerors did in fact mine; sinking deep shafts into the earth, shattering ore by heating it with fire and then dousing it with cold water.

Such processes for extracting became unnecessary when the then rich and powerful Iberian empire "discovered" and conquered the extravagantly wealthy Aztec and Incan empires of the new world.

store and Chinese Museum. Chinese and pioneer artifacts are featured among the museum's collections. Other historic structures include an impressive brick-and-store Chinese gambling house (casino) built in 1855 and the brick Wells Fargo office (now part of the Community Hall), built in 1853.

Also among these best-preserved buildings is the Schallhorne Blacksmith and Wagon Shop, built circa 1870.

FIDDLETOWN's fame must, in part, rest on its name. Founded by Missourians in 1849, it was named by an elder in the group who described the younger men as "always fiddling". The name FIDDLETOWN persisted for almost thirty years. In 1878 at the insistence of one Judge Purinton, so the story goes, who had become known in SACRAMENTO and SAN FRANCISCO, much to his embarrassment, as the "Man from Fiddletown", the name was changed. Eventually, however, the old name, whose charm was quickly recognized by Bret Harte and immortalized by him in *An Episode in Fiddletown*, was restored in the 1920s.

"I shall never forget the delight with which I struck and worked out a crevice. It appeared to be filled with a hard gravel, which I took out with my knife, and there at the bottom, strewn along the whole length of the rock, was bright yellow gold, in little pieces about the size of a grain of barley. Oh, how my heart beat! I sat still and looked at it some minutes before I touched it".
-Journal of Edward Butlum; written while prospecting near Hangtown (Placerville), 1848.

Just nine miles south of Sutter's Mill, PLACERVILLE by turn, followed only MORMON ISLAND as Gold Country's first "camp". Settled in 1848 and named after placer mining (a process that involves removing gold from ancient or active streambeds by "washing" it using either a pan, longtom, or sluice box), the camp had originally been called Dry Diggin's, because of it's scarcity of water (needed to wash the gold-laden soils). Three prospectors - Daylor, Sheldon, and McCoon - made the area's first strike, taking in $17,000 their first week!

Nevertheless it was not until the mid-nineteenth century, following the dawning of the age of the common man amidst the birth of a nation that enshrined democratic values, that the world witnessed its first true gold rush.

California! 1848! The world came rushing in! Free men, all, by virtue of their arrival in this remote wilderness. Suddenly "common men" were looking for gold everywhere

And they found it: in Nevada, British Columbia, Utah, Alaska, Colorado, Australia!

In the 40 years following discovery of California's treasure, more gold poured into the coffers of the world than had been produced in the previous four centuries.

It was gold discovered near Johannasberg, South Africa in 1888 that reigns supreme as the biggest bonanza of all time. Not surprisingly that nation today leads the world in gold production.

Nonetheless the *first* rush began and continues in the Golden State of California.

PLACERVILLE

News of that strike spread quickly. Dry Digging's rapidly became one of the most prosperous camps in the Mother Lode and subsequently one of the most important towns in the Sierra Nevada.

Frequently thereafter many a fortunate argonaut would strike a *bonanza* (rich pocket) of gold ore! Throughout that first summer following Marshall's gold discovery Dry Diggin's became the great rallying point for many of California's first treasure hunters. American's just in from the states, Spanish Californians, deserters from army posts and sailing vessels up and down the coast - a rag tag assemblage of distinct cultures, uniform, and styles - they were described by one as "the happiest set of men on earth".

Crime, as elsewhere throughout California in 1848, among this happy mob was virtually nonexistent. Tools and equipment were left to mark an individuals "claim" without the slightest fear of theft.

Here too the developmental formula for many a Gold Country mining camp was established: that being first as a true tent "city" of canvas, suceeded by the literal "thrown-up" wood frame boomtown (usually thereafter burned down by an out-of-control fire) and subsequently a re-constructed city primarily of adobe, stone or brick with iron shuttered doors and windows.

Among these foothills of the Sierra millions of gold nuggets, having been set free from a myriad of sources by the annual snowmelt in the high sierras, lay in stream beds or on shoals just waiting to be discovered. Nevertheless, hauling the gravels of Dry Diggin's down to running water to slosh in a pan was hard work.

PLACERVILLE holds the onus distinction as the birth-place of crime in the Mother Lode when unscrupulous newcomers unwilling to *work* took to mining gold dust not from placers but from more honorable, industrious miners.

Following one such particularly brutal crime in 1849, a hastily impaneled citizen's jury met to determine the fate of the accused. When the question was asked, "What shall be done with them?" Someone shouted, "Hang them!"

The majority voted in agreement. And so it was that the first known hanging in the Mother Lode was carried out.

The precedent having thus been set, hanging became the prescribed penalty throughout Gold Country for breaking Miner's law. Overnight Dry Diggin's became known as "Hangtown".

By 1854 *Hangtown* had become the third largest city in California! The local citizenry demanded that a more dignified name be bestowed upon their community. And so Hangtown was given the more distinguished name of PLACERVILLE that same year at the time of its incorporation.

PLACERVILLE owes its enduring success not to gold however or to forty-niner's lore, but rather to its role as a strategic communications and transportation corridor. This was the first service-oriented stop west of the Sierra for many who braved those early crossings of the Overland Trail. The town itself acquired the first telegraph in the West (in 1853), and later served as a major Pony Express Station. Following the Gold Rush, further income was derived from the stream of prospectors passing through on their way back across the Sierra to the

silver bonanzas of Nevada's Comstock Lode. Today US Highway 50, this now modern-day thoroughfare carries the adventurer to scenic splendor and a myriad of recreational opportunities at Tahoe, American's largest alpine lake. In South Lake Tahoe, where interstate 50 enters Nevada "territory", one will discover that the nightlife and gaming tradition of both the Comstock and Mother Lode lives on in what are today world-class gaming parlors and casinos.

Amid this wild atmosphere of fortunes made and lost overnight a few of PLACERVILLE's early residents managed to make, hold onto and build upon their *instant* riches; among them Mark Hopkins and Collis P. Huntington (both shopkeepers-turned-railroad tycoons) and one Philip D. Armour (future king of meat processing).

Another of Placerville's most famous citizens was J. M. Studebaker, a wheelwright who stuck to his trade instead of mining. From 1853 to 1858 Studebaker manufactured wheelbarrows for the miners at his shop at 543 Main Street (a plaque marks the location). With about $8,000 in savings (a tidy sum in 1859) he returned to Southbend, Indiana, where he and his brothers built what became the largest

FRONTIER JUSTICE

SOURDOUGH

A baking tradition born of the California Gold Rush was the now-famous sourdough bread.

Traditionally, a miner who had the foresight to save a starter piece of dough with which to leaven the following day's bread would discover that his dough had fermented overnight, giving the baked bread a distinctive "sourdough" taste.

The term "sourdough" also came to be used to describe an *experienced* prospector.

pioneer wagon factory in the world (and later served as the foundation for the Studebaker Automobile Corporation).

Today the seat of El Dorado County, most of *old* PLACERVILLE has been long since modernized. Still its street pattern, based on the trails marked off by miners' pack mules, remains. And if you look at the stores from the rear, away from the neon of new facades, you can find the town's true age revealed. Start your explorations by paying a visit to the Placerville Museum at 524 Main Street where docents will be happy to direct you to this charming mountain settlements surviving Gold Rush treasures.

There remain a number of historic buildings in the main business district; most notably the Pony Express building on Sacramento Street, just off Main Street (originally a harness shop when first built in 1858). A Pony Express historical marker can be found in the alley behind the building. The old City Hall is still standing. It was built in 1862 from funds donated by emigrant Jane Stuart, a true female "cowboy" who gained acclaim by driving herds of horses westward across the plains and over the Sierra to California to be sold here. The Cyrus Bales Building (erected in 1853) at 248 Main Street, Adams Express office (built in 1856) at 435 Main, Wells Fargo office (erected in 1856) at 437 Main, Smith & Nash hardware (built in 1856) at 441 Main and Pearson Soda Works (1859) at 594 Main Street are but a few of PLACERVILLE's many heirlooms.

The historic Cary House, where Mark Twain once lodged and where Horace Greeley delivered an historic address to the miners in 1859 stands at 300 Main Street. The site of the original Hangman's Tree is close by. The old Hangtown bell, used to call out the vigilantes as well as volunteer firemen, now stands at the intersection of Bedford and Main streets.

To visit Big Cut, one of the area's richest ore deposits, follow Big Cut Road southeast of town. At the top of the hill one can see how hydraulic nozzles cut away the cliffs to get at a reputed million dollars in gold an acre! Mining continued at Big Cut until 1900.

In Bedford Park, one mile north of town on Bedford Avenue, California's only city-owned, open to the public gold mine, Gold Bug Mine, affords visitors the unique experience of donning hard hat and walking into a *real* gold mine. Two shafts, 114 feet and 362 feet respectively, are lighted and open for self-guided tours. Also, check out a gold pan and sift the gravel of Little Big Creek, or drive up the hill to view the stamp press mill. This whole area was once the scene of feverish mining activity. In addition, Gold Bug Park offers picnicking facilities and hiking trails.

Of special note in old Hangtown is the El Dorado County Museum located west of town at the entrance to the County Fairgrounds. Here among other treasures one can see "Snowshoe" Thompson's ten-foot skis; a finely appointed concord stage coach and one of Studebaker's wheelbarrows!

Just south of PLACERVILLE off Highway 49 stands all that remains of El Dorado County's namesake. EL DORADO actually began as a stop along the Emigrant Trail. It's Nevada House served as a trading post and remount station on the Pony Express route. Not named or incorporated until the forty-niners arrived in 1849 and 1850, EL DORADO subsequently became a busy center of mining and commerce and home, temporarily at least, to several thousand miners.

The Wells Fargo Express office is today a local restaurant. Noteworthy murals on the inside walls depict the main street of town as it appeared in the 1850s.

SHINGLE SPRINGS, bisected by U.S. Highway 50, west of PLACERVILLE, today is much more involved in serving the commuting motorists from SACRAMENTO than in preserving an air of antiquity. A marker at the location of a fine, old native stone building at the west end of town (see photo, back cover) designates that historic structure as the town's original shingle mill (built in 1849). SHINGLE SPRINGS was named for the cool spring that flowed near a shingle mill. Several other structures of note are in the process of being restored and converted into small shops. Mining commenced here in 1850. Surrounding gulches were dotted with cabins, a few of which still brave the elements of time.

Nearby, along Green Valley Road, sits RESCUE. Originally the site of the Green Valley Ranch (in 1850), RESCUE later served as yet another remount station for the Pony Express. Today it is a picturesque collection of buildings dating back to the mid 1800s when RESCUE was primarily a stage stop. A few tables in a small park make it an attractive location for a picnic.

On a summit seven miles northwest of PLACERVILLE, well off the beaten path, along Gold Hill and Cold Springs Road stands the ruins of the old town of GOLD HILL. Roofless walls of a sandstone building bearing the date 1859 mark the site of this onetime thriving mining camp. After the first flush of mining had subsided, Japanese emigrants started the short-lived Wakamatsu Tea and Silk Farm Colony here in 1869.

"Snowshoe" Thompson

Today the name of a popular brand of sportswear, in fact Snowshoe Thompson (born John A. Thompson) was one of the truly heroic figures to emerge from the Gold Rush.

As a child Thompson emigrated to America with his parents from their homeland of Norway. As with many Scandinavians, the Thompson family was compelled by the call of freedom and opportunity. Settling to farm in the Midwest, young Thompson nevertheless could not resist the call of "instant riches" echoing across the continent from California.

At age 24 he set out for the gold fields. It was in and around Placerville where he exhausted his spirit and his strength placer mining. Success as a prospector eluded him. Downslope stretched the magnificent Central Valley with its familiar world of the farm. Retreating to that world to earn his "bread and beans" the young Norseman nevertheless longed for life in the mountains he had grown to love.

When word reached Thompson that the United States Postal Service was in search of a carrier for the high Sierra crossing, he dropped his plow, fashioned a crude pair of skis and showed up again in Placerville to apply for the job. John was twenty-nine.

From that day in 1856 until nearly twenty years later in 1876 Thompson delivered the mail across the Sierra Nevada between Placerville and Nevada's Carson Valley. His trip routinely took him three days over and two days back. While never actually employing Snowshoes, John traversed the high country on ten foot wooden skis. Often weighted down by medicine and supplies, in addition to the U.S. Mail, to reduce his load he generally traveled without blankets or firearms. He restricted even his food supply to a pocketful of salt pork and biscuits.

Never once did Thompson fail to get through. Over time his daily performance in completing what frequently proved a treacherous trip earned for him, perhaps more than any other, recognition as the embodiment of California's state motto, "Bring me men to match my mountains".

"One morning in January - it was a clear, cold morning, I shall never forget that morning — as I was taking my usual walk along the race after shutting off the water, my eye was caught with the glimpse of something shining in the bottom of the ditch. There was about a foot of water running then. I reached my hand down and picked it up. It made my heart thump, for I was certain it was gold."

-James Wilson Marshall/ "Discoverer" of California's Gold

COLOMA! This is where it all began. On a cold January morning in 1848, James Wilson Marshall picked up a few flakes of gold in the tailrace of John Sutter's sawmill and started the Gold Rush that forever changed the history of a nation and ultimately the economy of a whole planet.

Naturally COLOMA was the first of the many mining boomtowns. By summer of 1848 there were two thousand miners living here along the banks of the American River. That population swelled to ten thousand by the following year.

Virtually all of the new miners in the foothills started out at COLOMA before branching out in search of newer strikes.

Unlike boomtowns to follow COLOMA bypassed the initial "tent-and-canvas" stage as a mining camp, springing to life "full-blown" from lumber cut at Sutters Mill. By the end of that first summer following Marshall's discovery some 300 frame structures stood in the midst of what had little more than a year before been sylvan wilderness. Along COLOMA's main street stood the precedent-setting false front, wooden awning architecture that remained the "style" in California's Gold Country for the next half century.

It was also here at this remote boomtown that inflation hit the hardest. Picks and shovels sold for $50 each (a small fortune in 1849) and foodstuffs went for equally astronomical prices. It is little wonder then that Sam Brannon, the area's first shopkeeper, went on to become California's first millionaire!

Albeit the first boomtown, COLOMA certainly wasn't the longest lived. By 1852, there wasn't much gold left and a good part of the population had moved on to more productive "digs".

The now tranquil gold discovery site is preserved as part of 200-acre Marshall Gold Discovery State Historic Park. About seventy percent of the original townsite is actually incorporated within park boundaries. Among the few wood frame buildings still standing are St. John's Catholic Church and the Emmanuel Episcopal Church. Adobe structures include Chinese stores (built around 1856) and a blacksmith's shop complete with relic horse-drawn vehicles. In addition, two brick structures, Frank Beheart's gunshop (established in 1854) and the Robert Bell store (erected in 1855) are showcased.

Restorations throughout COLOMA continues. Buildings are marked for easy identification, and rangers on duty at park headquarters can provide a detailed map showing all points of interest. Also noteworthy at park headquarters is a replica of the first gold nugget discovered here (the original can be found in the Smithsonian Institute). It is mind-boggling when one considers that these tiny flecks of metal turned pastoral California into, as one historian put it, "a world gone mad."

By far the most imposing structure in COLOMA is the reconstruction of Sutter's Mill itself. It wasn't possible to rebuild the mill on the exact location of the original, since the American River has since altered its course substantially. The State was able to follow original construction techniques, however, right down to the hand-hewn beams and mortise-and-tenon joints. The electrically-powered sawmill operates regularly on weekends (weather permitting). Visitors can also watch ore being crushed at a nearby stamp mill.

On the hill behind town, an imposing bronze statue of James Marshall points to the site where he first discovered gold. A side road leads up to the monument. The more adventuresome can take a one-mile-round-trip hike to the statue by way of a restoration of the cabin Marshall lived in following his discovery of gold.

One of the best views of the Coloma Valley is from Mt. Murphy Road. At one time there was a cannon on top of this hill. It was used to signal the arrival of stagecoaches.

The supposedly haunted Vineyard House, south of the state park is today a restaurant. Its wine cellars were built around 1860.

Recreational activities here focus on the river. Today the American River near COLOMA has become the second most popular white-water-rafting site in the United States. Rapids run from tame to turbulent. Fishing in the South Fork of the American River is mediocre at best, but there are occasional catches of salmon and trout. At nearby Folsom Lake State Recreation Area, sports enthusiasts indulge in boating, water-skiing, swimming, and fishing.

The first modern-day argonauts in California's "mad" rush to riches were three former members of the Mormon Battalion. Employed temporarily at Sutters Fort, it was in late February of 1848 when they received word from a "brother" employed at Sutters Mill regarding Marshall's gold discovery.

Enroute to COLOMA, at an exposed sand bar remembered ever after as MORMON ISLAND the three Mormon elders discovered far richer placer deposits than anything being recovered at the mill. Soon MORMON ISLAND became Gold Country's *first* mining camp.

In 1856, the settlement was razed by fire. A century later saw the creation of Folsom Dam and Folsom Lake inundated what little remained of the historic locale. Today a state historic landmark on the shores of the reservoir stands near the sight of the former settlement.

◆

LOTUS, near COLOMA, lives a quiet existence with few reminders of its earlier glory days. Originally named MARSHALL in honor of the gold discoverer, the settlements old schoolhouse (still standing) opened in 1869. Today it is a private residence. Adam Lohry's red brick general store and family home (both constructed in 1854) currently houses a restaurant. Atop a nearby hill, a small cemetery contains headstones dating from the 1850s.

About a mile beyond town, rafters camp overnight between shooting the rapids of the American River.

◆

At PILOT HILL the only surviving building of interest is in fact one of the most interesting buildings in Gold Country. The imposing three-story Louisiana plantation-style Bayley House, stands in regal ruin alongside State Highway 49. Alonzo Bayley finished the house in 1862.

The town itself got its name from the "pilot" fires set on this, the area's highest hill, to guide pathfinder John C. Fremont's party safely down to this valley from the snowy heights of the high Sierra.

◆

Just off Highway 49, on Highway 193, GEORGETOWN, partly due to its location off the beaten

AMERICAN RIVER RAFTING

Photo by Ed Cooper

PLACER COUNTY COURTHOUSE

path, still bears the look of the mining frontier. One of the first things that strikes visitors to this handsome mountain town is its inordinately wide main street. A full 100 feet across, it was so designed as a sort of built-in fire prevention method following a particularly disastrous blaze that leveled the original tent city in 1852. Even side streets here are wider than usual (60 feet across) hypothetically to keep fire from jumping block to block.

GEORGETOWN got its start in 1849 when George Phipps and a party of sailors worked the stream below the present townsite and subsequently struck it rich. The camp was first named Growlersburg, because the sailors joked that large nuggets "growled" in the miners' pans. By 1855 nearly 3,000 treasure hunters were enjoying the "cultural life" in newly christened GEORGETOWN, which by then included both a town hall and theater. At its peak GEORGETOWN gained the accolade "Pride of the Mountains". Much of that old character is preserved here today with its many fine brick buildings built post-fire yet still dating back to the mid to late 1850s.

The Balsar House, a former three-story hotel and dance hall (erected in 1859), became the town's Opera House in 1870, then later the I.O.O.F. Hall in 1889, at which time the top floor of the building was removed. The Old Armory (1862) boasted a single door and no windows; the Shannon Knox House (oldest building in town) was constructed not of brick but rather of lumber shipped around the Horn, a sort of prefab predecessor (not altogether uncommon in those earliest days of settlement and in along the West Coast). The American Hotel is another picturesque survivor, as is the Georgetown Hotel (formerly the Nevada House).

◆

> *"There was very little law, but a large amount of good order; no churches, but a great deal of religion; no politics, but a large number of politicians; no offices, and strange to say for my countrymen, no office seekers. Crime was rare, for punishment was certain."*
> -Richard Oglesby Argonaut and later governor of Illinois

In Auburn the adventurer witnesses our quiet meanderings along what must be classified as relatively remote Highway 49 suddenly joined by today's world, as for the first time the historic route is bisected by a *freeway*: And not just any freeway, but in fact Interstate 80, one of America's major transportation corridors.

Upslope, above Gold Country, sits the scenic wonders and unlimited recreational opportunities of alpine Lake Tahoe. Beyond stretches the vast high plains, deserts and mountains of Nevada and the Great Basin. Many a hardy forty-niner pioneered this route in their determination to strike it rich in California's goldfields. What an adventure! "Any man who makes a trip by land to California deserves to find a fortune," wrote one argonaut. Most would in fact return home, or stay, with only the experience of the adventure itself as their reward. Yet, what a rich reward that must have been. In fact, for most forty-niners, the adventure alone proved to be, in and of itself, treasure enough for a lifetime.

It was in the spring of 1848 that a party of gold-seekers, organized by one Claude Chana in company with three fellow Frenchmen and some twenty-five native Americans, headed out across the foothills from the Sacramento Valley for Sutter's Mill. This first night out, on May 16, 1848, they camped by a stream at what came to called Auburn Ravine. Chana tried the gravels for gold and in his first pan found three sizable nuggets! Mining operations commenced immediately.

During the summer that followed, the gravels at North Fork Dry Diggings, as the camp was first called, yielded great wealth to those who made the effort to cart the pay dirt to the stream below. It was common place for a miner to wash out $1,000 to $1,500 a day. One account tells of four or five cartloads producing $16,000 in a single day! By 1850, fifteen hundred miners were busy digging in Auburn Ravine.

The name AUBURN first appeared in November of 1849, when a large group of miners who had come cross country with a Volunteer regiment from Auburn, New York arrived in the area. This busy little settlement of what was then Sutter County, was elected to serve as county seat in 1850 and sustained as such the following year when Placer County was formed.

After surface placers were exhausted, hardrock quartz mining kept the town booming. Yet, as with PLACERVILLE, it wasn't gold that built this modern city. From the outset AUBURN's location has made it a natural transportation corridor: both Interstate 80 and the Southern Pacific Railroad today passing through the community itself. AUBURN'S importance as a freight distribution point and supply center was assured with the arrival of the Central Pacific Transcontinental Railway in May of 1865. No longer dependent on gold mining for

FROM ADVENTURE TO INDUSTRY

Gold mining in California at first was a relatively unsophisticated process. Early arrivals found their treasure in alluvial deposits, or "placers" which lay close to the surface of the earth. The first forty-niners needed only to dig up likely "pay dirt" with pick and shovel, and wash away the lighter sand, clay and gravel in a pan or rocker.

The introduction of a sluice enabled miners to enlarge the scale of their operations, simply by shoveling larger amounts of "pay dirt" into a long trough through which a steady stream of water was directed. The fortune seekers were able to process more placers faster. Sluicing required large quantities of water which often had to be funneled through means of elaborate ditch work or flumes, all of which led to the invention of hydraulic mining.

By gathering together tremendous amounts of water and directing it through the nozzle of a hose, the pressure thus created tore the gold ore loose from hillsides. Environmentally unsound in the extreme, nevertheless this highly effective method of extracting gold ore persisted until outlawed prior to the turn of the century.

Gold ore is extracted from veins found in quartz by removing the rock and then having it crushed by means of a stamp mill. Mercury would then often be applied to help gather up the gold from the powder thus created.

As such *hardrock* mining operations grew larger; tunneling ever deeper into the earth, big industry stepped in to process the gold.

No longer feasible to produce cost effectively as individuals, the independent argonaut, as forty-niners were called, gave way to corporate giants which today conduct nearly all gold mining operations worldwide.

Today most newly found gold is used to produce jewelry (over 800 tons a year) and in dentistry (over 50 tons per year). The balance is applied by industries of all kinds for the production of everything from computer circuitry to radiation shielding on astronaut's helmets.

its economic survival AUBURN continued to flourish long after the gold gave out.

At NEWCASTLE, downslope from AUBURN on I-80, restored structures originally built to serve as depot for the First Transcontinental Railroad today house various local businesses (a state historic landmark identifies the location as today's Southern Pacific Depot).

Yet a few miles further west ROSEVILLE serves as the largest railroad marshalling yard west of the Mississippi (now operated by the Southern Pacific Railroad).

AUBURN today is known as California's "three story town." The modern commercial expanse of this city is built atop a hill along the town's "third-story" level. Because the business district migrated uphill over the years, the early buildings lying below at the town's "second story" level have been left relatively unmarred and untrammeled by modern commerce. The Old Town located here, with its fine collection of false front Gold Rush era architecture marching staunchly up the hill, is today preserved as a National Historic Landmark. An old town Auburn walking tour guide is provided free for the asking, from the local Chamber of Commerce. Look for the toylike, four-story firehouse, the Wells Fargo Office and the oldest continuously operated post office in the West (opened in 1849).

At the bottom of the ravine sits AUBURN's "ground floor" level. Little remains aside from a few half hidden foundations to indicate to the explorer that a full fledged boomtown, manned by hundreds of argonauts abandoning placers at nearby Sutter's Mill in droves, stood on this very site. An impressive monument to those men who, without intending to, set into granite bedrock the foundations of the impressive city we see today, marks the spot.

Indeed one of the largest and most beautiful cities in Gold Country, locally noteworthy buildings are also located up top, along Lincoln Way and High Street (i.e. St. Luke's Church, Kaiser Brewery, the Masonic Temple and Methodist Church—all built during the 1850s).

Centerpiece of AUBURN is the elegant Placer County Courthouse. Completed in 1894 it was recently restored at a cost of six million dollars. With its impressive capitol dome and four-sided matched entrances, each adorned with Greek pediments, it is among the most photographed and arguably the most striking building in all of Gold

Country. Courts are housed on the upper floors, while ground level rooms house the outstanding Placer County Museum. A must see for anyone touring the region, visitors experience meticulously restored sheriffs and county clerk's offices, and exhibits tracing AUBURN's extraordinary history back to the days of the Maidu Indians. Adjacent to the courthouse, the Bernhard Museum Complex affords visitors a tour through a fully-furnished Gold Country residence typical of the late 19th century. An 1854 winery is also located here.

Also of interest and open daily, the Gold Country Museum at Gold Country (Placer County) Fairgrounds affords exhibits of natural history collections and mining era memorabilia, Chinese and Indian artifacts, and interesting reconstructed settings depicting the life-style of the men who worked this region's mines.

—————— ◆ ——————

On the ridge above AUBURN (along I-80) lies FOREST HILL; a once prosperous mining and trading center during the early 1850s. Gold was first discovered here in 1850, but the boom did not really start until the Jenny Lind Mine was opened in 1852. This famous mine alone produced over a million dollars in gold by 1880, while the area around FOREST HILL produced in excess of $10 million!

One of the best-preserved hydraulic nozzles in the Gold Country is on display here near the community firehouse. Still surviving is a small collection of old businesses, traditional false-front buildings fronted by typical wooden sidewalks.

The Langstaff General Store, oldest building in FOREST HILL, served this community for over a hundred years. It was first opened in 1859 by the Garrison family and was operated continuously as a store until its closing in 1971. In fact, the unique institution of every mining camp and boomtown was its supply depot or general store. A sort of combination saloon, grocer's, hardware and social hall, behind the counter (which generally served as a bar as well) were stacked every conceivable item imaginable literally from pick and axe to caviar.

Coin being scarce, forty-niners generally paid for their "possibles" with a pinch of gold dust carried on their persons in a small leather satchel. Until World War II, gold was still exchanged for groceries here at Langstaff General Store. The Assay scales remain resting on a shelf near the cash register.

◆

Rich deposits of gold-bearing gravel along an ancient stream bed yielded $6 million worth of bullion and enabled GOLD RUN to boom right up to the court-imposed end of hydraulic mining in 1884. The town was founded by O.W. Hollenbeck in 1854 and was first called Mountain Springs.

Only the little shingled Union Church, with its shiny new roof, remains as a memento of the Gold Rush Era. The church was one of the many houses of worship in Gold Country financed by miners' contributions.

Throughout Placer County as elsewhere in Gold Country, names bestowed upon camps and towns now vanished are often all that remains: wonderful ridiculous names that speak to us of the forty-niner's sense of humor: Shirt Tail Canyon, You Bet, Last Chance, Deadman's Bar, Ground Hog's Glory, Milk Punch Bar, Humbug Bar, Ladies Canyon, Hell's Delight....If only the pines and rocks of these beautiful Sierra sites could speak!

◆

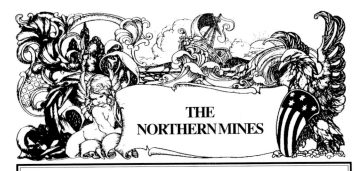

THE NORTHERN MINES

Whereas, when in the course of human events it becomes necessary for a people to protect themselves against starvation, when they are at the mercy of soulless speculators, we deem it right to act in self defense, and demand provisions for our need at prices we are able to give. Therefore, we declare,

That in consequence of impassable roads we are short of supplies necessary to support human life. That merchants refuse to sell at reasonable prices. That there are abundant supplies in San Francisco which speculators are holding for exorbitant prices. Therefore, be it

Resolved, that appealing to High Heaven for justice, we will go to San Francisco and obtain the necessary supplies - peaceably if we can, but forcibly if we must.

-Resolution drafted out of desperation by Grass Valley miners in 1851.

Execution of this proclamation never occurred as there was no money for travelling expenses.

FRATERNAL LODGES

One of the things that impresses visitors to Gold Country is the number of lodge-hall buildings almost always included amongst the best-preserved structures in most former mining communities. These buildings not only attest to the sound building practices of the lodge brothers, but they also reflect their importance as the result of a Gold Rush phenomenon: the need for companionship.

The strongest of the fraternal organizations in the eastern United States - particularly the Masons and International Order of Odd Fellows - sanctioned California lodges early in 1849 to help any of the brethren who might get into trouble far from home. Such fraternities quickly spread throughout the gold fields. New lodges opened with each new strike. Organizers had very little trouble recruiting new members, since the boys so far from home readily jumped at every chance to help overcome the lonely life in the mines. Those who struck it rich gave freely to building programs, with the result that lodge halls were made of the finest building materials.

To accommodate forty-niners without ties to a lodge the E. Clampus Vitis Society (headed by a grand noble Humbug) was born. Unique to California's Gold Rush, this rip-roaring "party" lodge was organized for the express purpose of "poking fun" at legitimate fraternal organizations. "Secret meetings" were little more than excuses to get together and have a good time.

Nevertheless these boys contributed heavily to the welfare of each other, individuals in need outside the lodge and to many a just and worthy cause.

Reborn and vibrant today, the E. Clampus Vitis Society has focused its energies on memorializing sites of historical significance throughout the golden state by funding monuments to identify them. They are still reportedly among the best "party throwers" in California.

Just downslope from historic Truckee and the splendor of Lake Tahoe, along Interstate 80 north of Highway 49 sits DUTCH FLAT. One of the most endearing hamlets in the northern mines, DUTCH FLAT, boasts a number of significant historic buildings, as well as pleasant residential areas that lend to this community its special character.

A German (not Dutch) argonaut, Joseph Dorenbach, and several of his countrymen started placer mining what hereafter became known as DUTCH FLAT in 1851. From 1854 to 1883 theirs was one of the principal gold mining towns in the State. Millions of dollars in bullion were extracted here (one nugget alone having been worth more than $5,000). The "diggins" lay over the hill about 100 feet north of town in rugged man-made canyons (the results of hydraulic mining).

It was also here that Theodore Judan and Dr. P. W. Strong made the original subscriptions to build the first transcontinental railroad. Until the railroad had pushed its way farther up the mountains to the town of CISCO, DUTCH FLAT was an important stage stop on both the Donner Pass and Hennessy Pass routes. When the railroad did come to town this tiny mountain camp was thrown into the national limelight as the namesake for the Central Pacific's "Dutch Flat Route". At the height of its prosperity the town supported two hotels and dozens of other small businesses. Visitors can pick up a sizeable amount of information about these surroundings at the Gold Drift Museum located at 32820 Main Street. Structures not to be overlooked include the I.O.O.F. Hall and Masonic Temple (1856), Dutch Flat Hotel (1851), Methodist Church (1861) and Dutch Flat Trading Post (built in 1854).

◆

Following Highway 49 north out of Auburn the traveler enters GRASS VALLEY. Arguably the most important "historic" Gold Rush town in all of California, it was here that gold mining hit its peak as an *industry*. This was not a camp where independent miners found nuggets of gold with pick and pan, but rather the area where corporate America with its big money and big machinery moved in to efficiently extract as much gold as possible from mineral-rich earth. The most important "ruins" left around GRASS VALLEY are not small brick businesses or quaint Chinese quarters, but rather headframes and incline shafts

of the big mining complexes that once employed thousands of miners here.

Nevertheless GRASS VALLEY's first big strike came about much as it had in any other mining camp - that being simply by accident. A farmer by the name of George Knight stubbed his toe while out after dark searching for his missing cow. In the moonlight he noticed a glimmer of shining metal. Knight took the piece of rock home and crushed it. A few minute's work with the gold pan revealed that the rock was indeed gold-bearing quartz - not the first discovered in Gold Country but by far a most important find.

The news of Knight's discovery brought miners in droves. Prospectors became quickly disheartened however when they came to realize that the gold here lay, not on top of the earth in placers, but deep beneath it in quartz veins. The solution was obvious: *dig*! To do so required great working capital. Those financially positioned to become investors did so and were rewarded literally with untold riches. Evidence the beautiful Bourne Cottage, Country home to the principal owner of the EMPIRE MINE (his primary residence, Filoli, south of San Francisco, is recognized around the world as the home of the fictional Carringtons from television's long-running primetime soap "Dynasty").

Those who were not so positioned to take part became employees of the large corporate mining operations thus established. It was at GRASS VALLEY that for the first time the forty-niner put down his pick and pan and began punching a time clock.

Knight sold his rights to his mine in 1851 for a mere $350, considering himself ahead in the deal. He could not have known that by 1864 that mine would have yielded more than a million dollars in gold bullion.

When the big mining companies moved in they attracted important suppliers and peripheral industries. Subsequently GRASS VALLEY possessed a broad economic base that was very rare in the Gold Country. The business of hardrock quartz mining was raised to an art form here, with the hit-and-miss methods of adventurous prospecting being replaced by industrial techniques that required calculation and strategy rather than mere luck and brawn.

Soon within a mile or two of GRASS VALLEY could be found the Empire, North Star, Pennsylvania, Idaho-

Photo by Mark Gibson

THE GOLD FIELDS

NEVADA CITY

Lola

"OH THOSE GOLDEN SLIPPERS"

Lotta Crabtree, the little darling of the mining camps, began her career as a professional entertainer at the tender age of 8 when she toured Gold Country dressed in green knickers and green coat with matching high hat, singing Irish ballads and dancing to tunes she would come to make famous.

No doubt longing for their own children and siblings in a virtual all male world, the boys attending little Lotta's performances in droves, literally showered her with gold.

This is not to say that little Lotta didn't have talent. She had been schooled when little more than a toddler by none-other-than international socialite and entertainer extraordinare, (and "next-door-neighbor") Lola Montez.

Lotta brought natural-born talent to her rehearsals (and would go on to become no doubt Lola's greatest claim to fame). Lola brought technique and experience, and boy did she have both!

Maryland and Brunswick mines to name but a few. Hundreds of miles of tunnels and shafts were dug beneath GRASS VALLEY and neighboring NEVADA CITY. Mining continued here well into the 1950s, even experiencing somewhat of a resurgence as this publication goes to press.

Experienced hardrock miners, many of them from Cornwall, England, were subsequently recruited, to man the giant gold mining operations. Cornish miners carried down into the shafts their now famous meat-and-potato pies known as pasties. The men were fond of leaving bits of pastie behind for the rats whose presence they considered a blessing. Proving to be important air quality indicators, if methane were to begin building up the rats would start to die, alerting the miners to get out!

A fire in 1855 - probably the most disastrous of the many that ravaged Gold Rush camps - destroyed the nearly three hundred frame buildings that made up the original community of GRASS VALLEY. It is said that it was this particular blaze that inspired the development of the characteristic heavy masonry walls and iron shutters and doors which came to typify Mother Lode architecture.

In spite of its contemporary appearance GRASS VALLEY still exudes an aura of early mining days. Narrow, winding streets and several Gold Rush era structures remain. One such notable, the Lola Montez residence (actually a reconstruction), at the corner of Mill and Walsh Streets is now home to the Nevada County Arts Council. Nearby stands the home of Lola's protegee, Lotta Crabtree (238 Mill Street).

Main Street boasts the Holbrooke Hotel. It was built in 1862 around the Golden Gate Saloon. The saloon, first opened in 1852, is the oldest continuously operating saloon in Gold Country. The hotel's brick and fieldstone construction is an outstanding example of the architectural style of buildings erected during the Gold Rush.

To best recapture Grass Valley's "glory days" visit the Empire Mine. Today part of California's state park system, the tour offered here is one of the most rewarding available in Gold Country. The Empire Mine alone yielded more gold (nearly three and a half million ounces) than was subsequently produced by the entire Klondike Gold Rush in the Yukon. A high point of your guided expedition underground is a visit to the beautiful Bourne Cottage

Born Eliza Gilbert in Ireland in 1818, Lola, having become a sensation of sorts herself in the world of European theater, came to California in 1850 to dazzle the miners with her striking beauty and shocking spider dance.

Locating herself in Grass Valley together with her pet monkey and pet bear, Lola met and took under her wing little Lotta Crabtree.

Montez later struck out for even more remote but just as prosperous gold fields in Australia. Crabtree was smart enough not to accompany her, staying home in California where she grew ever more popular with the miners. The wholesome joy she conveyed made her the most beloved of all traveling entertainers in Gold Country. She went on to perform successfully as a stage actress both in San Francisco and New York.

The first American entertainer to become a millionaire, she left behind an estate valued at more than $4 million.

Lotta

---

above ground. Its clear-heart redwood rooms, all hand dressed and beautifully appointed with original furnishings, and outdoor formal English rose gardens (all the roses pre-1929 varieties) reveal this "cottage" to be in fact an elegant mansion, and today the pride of GRASS VALLEY itself.

———————◆———————

Along the only stretch of Highway 49 to have since become a freeway, commuters are transported from busy GRASS VALLEY to the Gold County gem of NEVADA CITY. One of the earliest towns in the northern mines, NEVADA CITY sprang to life when miners started working the placers along Deer Creek back in 1849. Originally called simply NEVADA, the "city" part was added later to distinguish it from the nearby territory (later state) that took the same name.

As with other Gold Rush towns, NEVADA CITY was razed by fire, rebuilt, burned, and rebuilt again, and burned again in 1856! This last conflagration caused the local citizenry to form fire companies and build three good firehouses (about time). Two are still in use by the NEVADA CITY fire department. The third today houses an outstanding museum.

NEVADA CITY is one of the most charming of all Gold Rush towns. Storybook-like (it's church spires reaching high above the pine trees and roof tops on the slopes of Deer Creek Ravine), beyond individual landmarks the scene, looking out across at it, can best be described as *picturesque*. If you drive the side streets, you'll find interesting vintage commercial buildings and Victorian homes. The early-day Gold Rush architecture is eye-catching and memory-provoking: broad balconies and roof turrets, mullioned windows and widow's walks, garden gazebos and picket fences. Best explored on foot, visitors can pick up a "walking tour" brochure from the NEVADA CITY Chamber of Commerce.

Broad Street is this town's main thoroughfare. Along it you'll find the venerable National Hotel (1856), the oldest continuously operating hotel in California. The establishment's Victorian dining room, historic tavern and period furnished guestrooms keep the ambiance and tradition of the Gold Rush alive. Continuing along Broad

Street you encounter Citizens Banks (1859), the Methodist Church (1864) and red brick Firehouse No 2.

In NEVADA CITY's business district, beginning at Main and Coyote Streets, is Ott's Assay Office and south Yuba Canal Building (1855). It was James J. Ott who first assayed the ore samples that led to the Comstock Silver Rush in neighboring Nevada territory (but that's another story).

Today Ott's Office is home to the Chamber of Commerce. The old Chinese section of NEVADA CITY was located on Commercial Street. Here you'll still find a few of the buildings built back in the 1860s. Coyote Street is named after coyote holes, small shafts used to get at the gold deposits buried deep in the gravels of old river beds. The American Victorian Museum, a captivating collection of Victoriana, occupies the Miner's Foundry on Spring Street. On Prospect Hill, the gingerbread-trimmed Red Castle is today an inn. The aforementioned Firehouse Museum today displays among its treasures relics of the infamous Donner Party and a complete alter from a Chinese Joss House.

NEVADA CITY continues to preserve and restore its heirloom architecture. The nineteenth-century Nevada Theatre, California's oldest theater, has been renovated and beautifully restored. Once the stage for artist and celebrities such as Mark Twain and later Jack London, today it carries on that tradition as a center of fine entertainment. Still other notable structures, such as the Searls building (which housed the law offices of three generations of the Searls family and serves today as a museum and library), have since undergone complete restoration. Gaslight fixtures have been installed along Broad Street. Quite a change from the days when miners were so eager for wealth that they in fact kept the city's streets pretty much torn up! A story is told of one angry merchant who demanded that a certain miner stop digging up the street in front of his shop. The miner refused, stating there was no law to prevent him from such action. "Then I'll make a law," replied the indignant merchant who promptly produced his revolver. Destruction of the streets was said to have halted!

At nearby Malakoff Diggings State Historic Park (fifteen miles northeast of NEVADA CITY) visitors can witness dramatically the damaging effects hydraulic mining had on the environment at this, the largest hydraulic gold mine in the world. Visitors will also learn how and why it was such a popular method of gold extraction until outlawed by the State in 1884.

━━━━━◆━━━━━

ROUGH AND READY (west of GRASS VALLEY on Highway 20), a quiet little village that belies its name, was founded by a band of Mexican War veterans who took the name from their ex-commander, General Zachary Taylor, "Old Rough and Ready" himself.

The settlement's greatest claim to fame came from its attempt at secession from the Union in 1850 in protest over the afore mentioned imposed miners tax. The town actually "returned" to the United States after only a few months, but technically the rebellion did not end until 1948 when "peace" was officially made with the federal government so that a post office could be opened.

Another one of the town's most famous incidents reflects the temper of Gold Rush times. It seems that an unfortunate miner was being buried when one of the "mourners" in attendance at the funeral service suddenly noticed some flecks of gold in the freshly turned earth at the gravesite. Before the preacher could finish the service he sensed that something was distracting those in attendance. "Boys, what's that?" he questioned. "Gold, by God," came the reply. Solemnly raising his hand he pronounced the services suspended and led the rush to stake a claim. The body of the unfortunate was subsequently consigned to ground "more hallowed" and obviously less rich.

During the 1850s there were more than three hundred frame buildings in this now-tiny town. Today three of Rough and Ready's oldest landmarks are its school house, the I.O.O.F. hall, and the blacksmith shop all dating back to the early 1850s. The Old Toll House, which charged from twenty-five cents to $3.00 to pass through, depending upon the weight of one's freight, now extracts revenues from motorists by the sale of antiques.

━━━━━◆━━━━━

"American Hill was covered with tents and brush houses, a few had put up cabins. At night the tents shone through the pines like great transparencies, and the sound of laughter, shouting, fiddling and singing startled those old primeval solitudes strangely. It was a wild, wonderful scene."

Forty-niner Ben Avery's description
of Nevada City in 1849

riving north along the final stretch of Highway 49 the modern day explorer leaves one of the busiest areas of Gold Country to approach its most remote.

In one of the highest and most rugged regions of the State, DOWNIEVILLE sits in a natural wooded amphitheater surrounded by lofty, pine-clad mountains.

Named for self-proclaimed " Major" William Downie who wintered here in 1849 (after building cabins in anticipation of a several month stay), Downie's party began prospecting simply to occupy their time. They were pleasantly surprised to find the region was in fact rich in gold. By the end of that first spring in the mountains "The Forks" (as it was then called) was growing rapidly as news of the rich strikes spread. By June, 1850, about five thousand men were established here.

These early argonauts *earned* their gold - working long hours in icy waters, with meager supplies, and suffering great difficulty acquiring lodging. The incoming trail was almost impassable for a good many months each year and commodities were both scarce and expensive. Shirts sold for $50, boots were $25 to $150 a pair, and potatoes cost $3 a pound (unheard of elsewhere for that era, even in Gold Country)!

Like many other camps along the forks of the Yuba, DOWNIEVILLE contributed its share of rich gold strikes like that of Tin Cup diggings where three miners had little trouble filling a cup with gold dust each day, or the 60 square-foot claim that yielded over $12,000 in eleven days, or the 25-pound nugget of solid gold taken two miles above the town.

Looking much like a toy village, its single avenue hemmed in between the rushing current of the Yuba River and the crowding slopes of the Sierra Nevada, eventually DOWNIEVILLE, for all of its remoteness, came to bare a veneer of civility. All of the accoutrements of civilization began to be packed in by mule train. At any of the "camps" fine dining establishments "men in open red flannel shirts with bare arms and exposed chests spread a fine linen napkin over their muddy knees and studied the bill of fare for half an hour before they could make up their minds what to order for dinner."

The acquired refinement of this high mountain enclave suffered a severe blow, however, when in 1851 a lover's quarrel resulted in murder. A rush to judgement saw the perpetrator of the crime, the beautiful Joseta (popularized in legend as Juanita), summarily executed by hanging. Shocked and infuriated, the citizenry of California pushed for legislation to outlaw against nearly a decade of vigilantism and "mob rule".

Fire and flood too have done their best to destroy this tiny mountain settlement; yet DOWNIEVILLE survives as one of the most entrancing locales in all of Gold Country. The old stone, brick, and frame buildings (many of which were built in the 1860s or earlier) face on quiet, crooked streets that once echoed with the clatter and rumble of freighters and the din that hundreds, sometimes thousands, of miners could raise when they came to town for a night of revelry.

On Main Street are the present-day Sierra County Museum (formerly a Chinese store and gambling house), the Hirschfelder Building, and the two-story brick-and-stone Craycroft Building (with its classic iron doors) all dating back to 1852. The multipurpose Craycroft Building has served as saloon, courtroom, jail, newspaper office, restaurant, Masonic Lodge and even a place of temporary refuge to which the ill-fated Joseta had fled.

On the south side of the Yuba River, the Masonic building, the Native Daughters Hall across the street, the Catholic and the Methodist Churches all date from the 1850s and 1860s.

A few blocks east of the museum, the site of Major Downie's original cabin is marked. Over by the courthouse are this town's infamous gallows. Other buildings, built in the 1860s, cling to the mountainsides above the river. Lovely vintage residential areas add to the luster of this jewel of the Sierra.

———◆———

Above DOWNIEVILLE, along near-perpendicular slopes, ALLEGHENY's houses balance precariously on hillside terraces. Streets are narrow and unpaved, winding down from one level to the next.

At the bottom of the ravine is Kanaka Creek, named after Hawaiians who made the first big gold strike here in May of 1850. Kanaka Creek, rich in gold ore, generated yet another boom to this primitive mountain country.

One exciting ongoing success story in Gold Country is ALLEGHENY'S famous Sixteen To One mine. Opened in 1896, it has operated continuously (except for a brief closure during the 1960s), producing millions of dollars in gold bullion! Acknowledged by the mining fraternity to be one of the most successful mining operations ever, its unusually rich, high-grade ore seems endless.

**SATURDAY NIGHT
IN THE MINES**

Following the old stage road from DOWNIEVILLE, the Mother Lode Highway sweeps upward past meadows and apple orchards. An occasional miner's cabin or farmhouse is seen before the traveler reaches SIERRA CITY. Here the towering Sierra Buttes overshadow a tiny mountain hamlet.

The Sierra Buttes Mine, whose tunnels reach all the way down to the river below, was first operated back in 1850. It subsequently produced some $17 million in gold. In 1852, the mountains had their revenge on this intrusion when an avalanche of ice and snow crushed every shack and tent in the tiny boomtown. It wasn't until 1858 that a permanent settlement emerged on the previously buried townsite. Other catastrophic snow avalanches would again occur in 1888 and 1889. Many were killed in each vengeance exacted by the mountains.

Most of the old structures left standing in town today date from the 1870s. The largest of these, the Busch Building, was built back in 1871. Wells Fargo was one of its early tenants.

SIERRA CITY's three story, tin roof-Zerloff Hotel was built in the 1860s. It is still operated by the same family which founded the institution during the Gold Rush. The hotel's saloon was but one of some twenty-two in operation during the glory days of the Gold Rush.

Take note of the unique fieldstone wall of SIERRA CITY's post office, where the side of an ore cart and related mining equipment have been used to create a unique and rusty bas-relief sculpture.

At Sierra County Historical Park and Museum just outside of SIERRA CITY, the local citizenry have transformed the ruins of the old Kentucky Mine into one of Gold Country's most noteworthy exhibits; affording visitors an outstanding "hands on" experience. Today the mine's ten stamp mills, a blacksmith shop, restored miner's cabin and charming museum are just a few of the "parks" amenities. An outstanding series of outdoor summer concerts help to fund the on-going restorations of the mine together with its attendant structures.

North of SIERRA CITY, a few miles west of Highway alternate 40, at JOHNSVILLE stands the best-preserved wood-constructed boomtown in the northern mines. JOHNSVILLE (in the center of what is today Plumas-Eureka State Park), as a mining camp was a latecomer, having been built in the 1870s by a company of London investors.

There are several historic buildings in various stages of collapse (among them an old church and fire house), making this spot an excellent subject for photographers. Visitors are advised to tread carefully, however, since most of the buildings are privately owned and/or unsafe. Plumas-Eureka State Park, open year-round, has a good collection of old mining implements and wagons. The State is currently working on a long-range program to restore the stamp mill of the Plumas-Eureka Mine together with some of the towns other historic buildings. Eureka mine's former bunkhouse and office have been transformed into park headquarters and functioning interpretive center.

A marker designates JOHNSVILLE as a pioneer ski area. SIERRA CITY, LAPORTE, JAMISON CITY, JOHNSVILLE and five other neighboring mining camps organized ski clubs, and held annual winter sport competitions here beginning in 1860. A century of sport skiing in California was subsequently commemorated in 1960, when the winter Olympics were held nearby at Squaw Valley. Today there exists a designated ski area; however, the park's major activities are hiking, camping, and fishing. State Highway 49 continues to parallel the North Yuba River, crossing alpine Yuba Pass, through SIERRAVILLE and LOYALTON before terminating in a whisper at tiny VINTON.

<u>CALIFORNIA'S SECOND GOLD RUSH</u>

Below the amber hills of Gold Country stretches the vast, fertile expanse of California's great Central Valley. Many a fortunate argonaut invested his "pay dirt" into this rich dirt, often reaping great rewards and ultimately setting into motion the second great gold rush for the golden state.

An agricutural bonanza, soon miners-turned-farmers were producing everything from alfalfa to almonds to oranges!

One favorite success story is that of the State's enterprising vintners. An unseasonal heat wave hit the great Valley, drying grapes on the vine and seemingly spelling disaster for the growers. In desperation they hauled their devastated crop to market in San Francisco offering it up as "Peruvian delicacies". Their ploy met with immediate success as the popularity of this "newly discovered" exotic treat spread throughout Gold Country and beyond: making Central Valley grape growers the "hit" of the season and giving birth to the California Raisin Industry.

GOLD MINERS

A.D.O. Browere, 1858, oil on canvas, *Anschutz Collection.*

Epilog

"It was in this Sacramento Valley that a great deal of the most lucrative of the early gold mining was done, and you may still see, in places, its grassy slopes and levels torn and guttered and disfigured by the avaricious spoilers of fifteen and twenty years ago. You may see such disfigurements far and wide over California—and in some such places, where only meadows and forests are visible—not a living creature, not a house, no stick or stone or remnant of ruin, and not a sound, not even a whisper to disturb the Sabbath stillness—you will find it hard to believe that there stood at one time a fiercely-flourishing little city, of two thousand or three thousand souls, with its newspaper, fire company, brass band, volunteer militia, banks, hotels, noisy Fourth of July processions and speeches, gambling halls crammed with tobacco smoke, profanity, and rough-bearded men of all nations and colors, with tables heaped with gold dust sufficient for the revenues of a German principality—streets crowded and rife with business—town lots worth four hundred dollars a front foot—labor, laughter, music, dancing, swearing, fighting, shooting, stabbing—a bloody inquest and a man for breakfast every morning—everything that delights and adorns existence—all the appointments and appurtenances of a thriving and prosperous and promising young city, —and *now* nothing is left of it all but a lifeless, homeless solitude. The men are gone, the houses have vanished, even the *name* of the place is forgotten. In no other land, in modern times, have towns so absolutely died and disappeared, as in the old mining regions of California.

"It was a driving, vigorous, restless population in those days. It was a *curious* population. It was the only population of the kind that the world has ever seen gathered together, and it is not likely that the world will ever see its like again. For, observe, it was an assemblage of two hundred thousand *young* men—not simpering, dainty, kid-gloved weaklings, but stalwart, muscular, dauntless young braves, brim full of push and energy and royally endowed with every attribute that goes to make up a peerless and magnificent manhood—the very pick and choice of the world's glorious ones. No women, no children, no gray and stooping veterans, —none but erect, bright-eyed, quick-moving, strong-handed young giants—the strangest population, the finest population, the most gallant host that ever trooped down the startled solitudes of an unpeopled land. And where are they now? Scattered to the ends of the earth—or prematurely aged and decrepit—or shot or stabbed in street affrays—or dead of disappointed hopes and broken hearts—all gone, or nearly all—victims devoted upon the alter of the golden calf—the noblest holocaust that ever wafted its sacrificial incense heavenward.

It was that population that gave to California a name for getting up astounding enterprises and rushing them through with a magnificent dash and daring and a recklessness of cost or consequences, which she bears unto this day—and when she projects a new surprise, the grave world smiles as usual, and says "Well, that is California all over".

(An excerpt from Mark Twain's <u>Roughing It.</u> Originally published by Harper & Brothers, New York, NY.)

Acknowledgments

We are indebted to many giving and talented individuals without whom this Gold Country portfolio would have been impossible to produce. First and foremost, I wish to express my gratitude to Mr. Robert Haydon and Mr. Paul Claiborne, Jr. for having provided the opportunity to create this wonderful piece and for their confidence and ongoing support of our enterprise.

Special thanks to Richard and Diane for seeing me through yet another journalistic odyssey.

Many thanks are due likewise to many state park rangers and docents and local travel writers, journalists and educators whose shared love for California and the Gold Rush in particular, helped us to bring the entire experience back to life.

Thanks also to a talented creative staff, both in Anaheim, as well as at Palace Press International in San Francisco who made certain that the vision conceived was delivered as projected.

And, thanks, Mom, as always for ever being there for me, my team and my friends. I love you.

Adam R. Collings

Adam R. Collings, Publisher
Gold Mountain Books

INDEX